Second Edition

A Guide to
Stock Control

ALBERT BATTERSBY
Fellow of Balliol College, Oxford

A

PUBLICATION

PITMAN PUBLISHING

Second edition 1970

Sir Isaac Pitman and Sons Ltd.
Pitman House, Parker Street, Kingsway, London, W.C.2
P.O. Box 6038, Portal Street, Nairobi, Kenya
Sir Isaac Pitman (Aust.) Pty. Ltd.
Pitman House, Bouverie Street, Carlton, Victoria 3053, Australia
Pitman Publishing Company S.A. Ltd.
P.O. Box 9898, Johannesburg, S. Africa
Pitman Publishing Corporation
6 *East 43rd Street, New York, N.Y.* 10017, *U.S.A.*
Sir Isaac Pitman (Canada) Ltd.
Pitman House, 381—383 *Church Street, Toronto,* 3, *Canada*
The Copp Clark Publishing Company
517 *Wellington Street, Toronto,* 2B, *Canada*

© Albert Battersby 1962, 1970

ISBN: 0 273 31566 8

Printed in Great Britain
By Ebenezer Baylis and Son Limited
The Trinity Press, Worcester, and London

GO—(MAN) 110

I dedicate this second edition
to those members of the National Health Service,
the Ambulance Service and the Police
without whose timely help
there would have been
no author to write it.

A.B.

Preface to Second Edition

When this book was first written, ten years ago, I prefaced it by drawing attention to stocks as a national problem, although the book was addressed then, as it is now, to the individual businessman. How has the situation changed in the last decade? Economic statistics are difficult to compile, so they are apt to be tardy and open to suspicion. The figures which follow have therefore been freely rounded off and although their source is a most respectable one,[1] they should be taken as only rough indicators of national trends: they are given in thousands of millions of pounds. In the five years following 1962, the country's total stocks and work in progress rose from 10 to 13, but some of this increase was undoubtedly due to monetary inflation. Indeed, the 13 thousand millions become 11·6 when revalued at 1958 prices. It is therefore worth our while to look at the *relative* increase—relative, that is, to production.

In the same period, the gross domestic product rose from 34 to 46 (still in thousands of millions of pounds), so from holding 3·7 months' stock nationally, we reduced to 3·4 months. The cynical reader will say, with some justification, that this only goes to show you can prove anything by statistics; the professional statistician will retort that statistics never in fact *prove* anything, but only fail to disprove an hypothesis. So choose your own hypothesis, economic wonder or economic blunder; meanwhile, any management scientist of experience will grant that much has been achieved already in the field of stock control, but much still remains to be done.

How, then, has this book been changed to meet the changes of the last decade? Fundamentally, not at all: it still aims to set out the first principles of stock control in a way which can be followed by the non-technical reader. It does, however, recognize that the modern businessman is becoming more sophisticated, as was exemplified by Sir Donald Stokes' description of his group as 'lean, fit and healthy'. The book defers to such sophistication by going rather more deeply into the problem; consequently, it is slightly longer. This, plus increased speed of inter-city railway services, no longer makes it

[1] *Monthly Digest of Statistics* (H.M.S.O.)

reasonable for me to claim that these pages can all be absorbed during a train journey from London to Manchester: perhaps it will now occupy the return journey as well.

An extra chapter has been added on calculating the size of storage space: it covers the difficult case in which both the supply (lead time) and demand (offtake) are variable.

The inventory of stocks including work-in-progress can make up a large proportion of the total assets of a limited liability company and thus affect the entire valuation of the company. The latter in turn affects the price of the company's shares in the stock market and acquires a special significance when a take-over bid is made or the assets subsequently made over. In the A.E.I./G.E.C. struggle and in the controversy about Pergamon Press, the valuation of stock was an important factor. I have therefore added a good deal of new matter on this topic to the chapter on management of stocks and am grateful to the Institute of Chartered Accountants in England and Wales for their generous collaboration. In particular, I acknowledge the freedom they have allowed me in quoting from their Recommendations on the subject.

All numerical examples in which money is involved have been altered to conform with Britain's new decimal currency. This has given rise to only one small difficulty; the original examples were carefully devised for ease of working, with calculations which fell easily into round numbers in the traditional currency. I have tried to retain this feature in the new currency in spite of the loss of exact divisibility by 3: in the main this effort has been successful, so I ask the reader to forgive the occasional slight inaccuracies (for example in Fig. 7), since they are trivially small. The reader will no doubt be as relieved as the author was to find that the later change to metric tons of 1,000 kilogrammes each will not affect the contents at all.

I have deleted the Bibliography in preference to revising it. This does not mean that the technical literature of the last decade contains nothing of interest, but that its importance is to the specialist rather than the reader towards whom this book is directed. Some useful elementary references are distributed throughout the text as footnotes: to them I would add a useful survey of the mathematics of the subject.[1] Also, there is now available a good review[2] of recent literature which is far more comprehensive than any survey I could offer here.

---

[1] S. EILON and W. LAMPKIN, *Inventory Control Abstracts* (Oliver and Boyd, 1968).

[2] J. H. MORRELL, *Problems of Stocks and Storage* (published for I.C.I. by Oliver and Boyd, 1967).

Although this book was originally written primarily as a guide for the manager rather than as a textbook for the student, it has in fact been widely used and recommended in the latter category. In deference to this usage I have included a few exercises at the end of some of the chapters (the answers will be found at the end of the book). These are designed not merely to increase the book's value as a textbook but to provide the conscientious executive with the opportunity to loosen up his 'mental muscles' as an aid to the absorption of new ideas. I also hope that the new appendix on the rapid calculation of square roots will be found useful.

January 1970   ALBERT BATTERSBY

I*

Preface to First Edition

I heard a Stock-dove sing or say
His homely tale, this very day ...
WORDSWORTH, *O Nightingale.*

The importance of good stock control cannot be too strongly emphasized. Not only does it concern the individual business, but indeed it affects the whole economy of the nation. The total stocks of material in Great Britain (including work in progress) are worth £9,000 million, of which about half is held in manufacturing industries (*Monthly Digest of Statistics*, H.M.S.O., November, 1960); there is evidence that this could be reduced, not merely by the odd one or two per cent, but more probably by ten or even twenty per cent.

Just after the war, this country borrowed one thousand million pounds from the United States to help our industrial recovery: a sum approaching this in magnitude may even now be lying stagnant in our material stocks, waiting to be applied to more productive ends.

The public became aware of stocks as a national problem in 1958, when the National Coal Board had to ask the Treasury for £55 million to finance the stockpiling of unsold coal, and again in 1959 when stocks had reached 35,400,000 tons and another £50 million were needed. More recently, Sir James Bowman was able to announce that 6,000,000 tons had been lifted from undistributed stocks in 1960, but—

... he recalled sadly that although the board was saving at the rate of about £50 millions a year compared with 1957, *the financial burden of stocking* and the need to cut out profitable opencast working had led to the price increase of 6s. 8d. a ton. (from *The Guardian*, 13th January, 1961; my italics—A.B.)

Not only do excessive stocks immobilize our capital resources: they can generate the so-called 'inventory recession' in the following way. A manufacturer of consumer goods finds his sales falling, perhaps as the result of a credit squeeze. He reduces his stocks of finished products *and* lowers his production rate; the orders which he places with his own suppliers reflect not only the decrease in sales but also the cut in stocks. The supplier reduces *his* production and stocks, and so the process goes on. A chain of this sort can be seen in the motor-car industry, extending back through the body manufacturers to the steel rolling mills and the blast-furnaces. By the time the original fall in sales reaches the basic industries, it has been magnified by successive reductions in stock into a recession—and that is not all. The producers are also the consumers; lessened activity cuts down their spending power and feeds back this effect as a further fall in the demand for consumer goods. The disturbance of the industries and the economy as a whole is costly.

Everyone concerned with stocks stands to gain by good stock control, not only in his own business but as a member of a prosperous nation. Its condition, like that of liberty, is eternal vigilance.

This book aims to show how that vigilance can and should be exercised. It is addressed to the non-specialist manager—the General Practitioner of business—rather than to my scientific colleagues. It does not purport to be a comprehensive textbook, although some of the techniques are described in detail in the first seven chapters, but rather aims to present a general picture of the state of the art at this moment. No mathematical symbols or equations are used—just plain English, line diagrams, and some arithmetic. I have also tried to avoid technical jargon as far as possible; only a few indispensable expressions are introduced and defined.

The early chapters discuss some fundamental principles and go on to build up a stock control system for a single mythical product. This is drawn from the chemical industry, reflecting my own experience, but could equally well be ball-bearings, beer, or bars of chocolate. I have emphasized throughout the dangers of blindly applying formulas without carefully examining all the assumptions beforehand.

The final chapters broaden out the pure theory of stock control systems and bring in the human beings who operate them. Without their co-operation, their goodwill and above all their common sense, the most ingenious and elaborate measures will fail. This, surely, is the essence of management—to begin with the dead facts and measurements of the past and use them to overcome the environmental and emotional disturbances of the future.

Finally, I have tried to make this a *readable* book—one which can be comfortably absorbed on a railway journey from London to Manchester. To achieve this, I have omitted footnotes and references except for a short bibliography, and have relegated to appendixes those passages which can be omitted at a first reading.

The material in this book is based for the most part on my lectures at the Institute for Engineering Production (University of Birmingham) and the Inventory Control Seminars of the British Institute of Management. The first half of Chapter 7 is a revision of an article originally published in *The Accountant* on 27th February, 1960. The questioning technique in Appendix 1 appeared in the *Work Study Journal*.

I am grateful to the editors of these journals for permission to reproduce this material; to Mr. Van Court Hare and *Management Technology* for Figs. 42, 46, and 47; to M. J. Melese and the International Federation of Operational Research Societies for Fig. 41; to Mr. Cyril Ray for the quotation in Chapter 1 and to Associated Electrical Industries Ltd. for permission to use the excerpts from their *Inventory Control Manual* in Chapter 10.

A.B.

Contents

CHAPTER 1

Problems, Principles and Policy

We first survey the plot, then draw the model;

Question surveyors, know our own estate,
How able such a work to undergo,
To weigh against his opposite; or else
We fortify in paper and in figures.
SHAKESPEARE, *Henry IV* (Part II).

A well-established business can suffer from obesity no less than a well-established business man. The latter has his weighing-machine, tape-measure and diet; the former has its financial and cost accounting and its stock control system. The man who wants to reduce his girth will consult an expert—his doctor. What can he do about the corresponding affliction in his business?

What we might call 'industrial obesity' is a widespread disease. Those who have studied the problem closely believe that in most manufacturing companies which do not yet practise scientific stock control, its introduction in a relatively simple and cheap form could reduce total stocks by about a quarter, with no loss of efficiency. More sophisticated control systems could do even better.

The wise fat man does not prescribe his own diet, but knows that he can talk more intelligently to his doctor if he understands the difference between carbohydrates and proteins. The wise business man will also seek professional advice ('question surveyors') on his stock problems; he will benefit from a prior knowledge of lead times, buffer stocks and the general 'anatomy' of stock control systems. Thus equipped, he will be able to combine this new understanding of stock control concepts with his wider business sense in seeing the obesity of his business, if it exists, as a problem which will yield to good management.

In general, management is concerned with planning and control, the former often being considered as part of the latter. Control is exercised in the *present* to achieve a plan previously drawn up for the *future*; both planning and control use theory which is the classified experience of the *past*. Thus management, with its whole emphasis

1

on a forward look, relies on the projection of the past into the future. There are several sorts of such management systems; they include not only stock or inventory control and production control but also statistical quality control and others. They tend to overlap in practice and it would be a mistake to think that they can be neatly isolated, each from the others. In fact, stock and production control are very intimately associated with each other and may even, to some extent, be associated with quality control also. Nevertheless, all are very much tied in with what has become fashionable to call the 'total system'. With this caveat, let us consider inventory control or stock control: it is convenient right at the outset to insert a note about nomenclature. You may regard 'inventory control', if you like, as simply an Americanism, in the same class as 'apartment' for flat and 'automobile' for car (and as some people might say rather unkindly, 'marketing' for sales) but the two *are* different and it is not merely as a matter of *cis-* and *trans*atlantic usage. Now 'inventory' in English means a list. If you let your house furnished and make an *inventory* of the contents it is just that, a list—and that is the meaning given by the dictionary. So stock control may be taken as applying to the individual stock centre and most of the theory that has been worked out does tend to deal with the individual and isolated stock centre. In this discussion, 'stock control' is also used in a general way which embraces both its individual and collective aspects. However there are very few companies, if any, that have simply one item of stock. If they did this one item would constitute their whole collection of stock centres, that is, their inventory. In practice, they are more likely to have a structure even more complicated than that shown in Fig. 1. This is a simplified version of an actual case, and shows a 'model' of the flows and stocks of materials in a factory, the latter classified according to their purpose as described later in this chapter. However, from the policy level, we may classify the individual stocks into two sorts, *accidental* and *purposeful*. Is it nonsense to talk about 'accidental' stocks? I think not. I once made a collection of statements by Chairmen of companies and sorted them into two piles. In the first pile the Chairman's comment on the figure for money tied up in stock went something like this: "Because our sales did not come up to expectations we have unfortunately been left with large accumulated stocks on our hands, but, of course, vigorous action is being taken to relieve this temporary setback, *etc., etc.*" In the other group the Chairman says: "Due to the enormous upsurge in our sales through the vigorous campaign prosecuted by our marketing department, *etc. etc.* it has become necessary to back these efforts with increased stocks of materials so as to provide customers

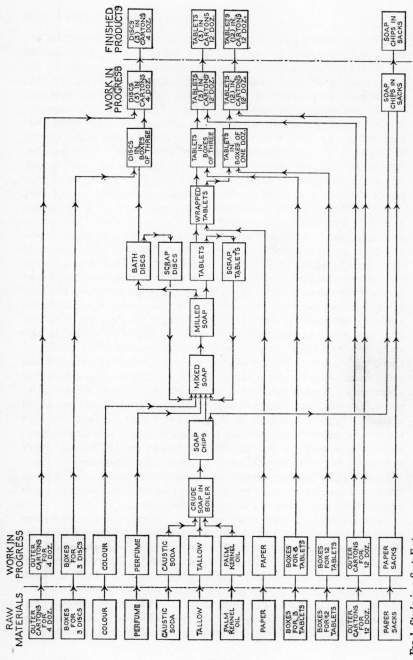

Fig 1 *Stocks in a Soap Factory*

with the service they deserve" (and so on). Stocks are *purposeful* when the latter statement is true, *accidental* otherwise. Now accidental stocks ought not to occur in a properly regulated company. All stocks should be planned for. Seventy years ago such a statement would have been nonsense because there was not the accumulated body of knowledge to allow stocks to be budgeted. There now is and it is not merely academic, because the technique of stock control has been widely applied in actual practice and has saved much money for those astute businessmen who are not afraid of innovation. Accidental stocks ought not to be there at all, they are not wanted. Any stock you have should be *purposeful*, should be *planned* and your policy should be to regulate this planned inventory in such a way that it is firstly, effective and secondly, efficient; we need to differentiate between the meanings of these two words. In order to determine the effectiveness and the efficiency of anything in business at all you first must define its *purpose*. The *effectiveness* is a measure of the extent to which that purpose is achieved, and is independent of the effort expended in doing so; the *efficiency*, however, takes into account the resources consumed in achieving the purpose, and that stock will be most efficient which best reconciles the maximum achievement with the minimum use of resources. Purpose, effectiveness and efficiency succeed each other in that order, and in this sequence lies the key to a successful inventory policy. We must begin, then, with *purpose*. Does a stock have a purpose? It has, and the recognition of it has brought about the revolution in our thinking about stock control which has taken place in about the last fifty years. The earliest paper ever written on stock control was published about 1915, so it was back in World War I that the first tentative steps were taken in expounding the theory (which was drawn from classical economics in the first place); then in the 1920's and 1930's the theory began to 'crystallize' into practical application.

In the most general terms, the purpose or function of a stock centre is defined as 'uncoupling' one process from another: this vague definition is set out in greater detail later.

Meanwhile, Fig. 2 shows an everyday example of a stock centre connected to an input and an output: an ordinary domestic bath. Its input comes from the taps and its output goes down the plughole; we cannot control the stock directly by pushing on its surface, but only by pulling out the plug or turning the taps on and off. We shall find later that this obvious point is fundamentally important in the study of stock control. The domestic bath is a simple analogy, but in some ways it is not a good one: the stock of water in it is an end in itself, whereas more often a stock is a means to an end. What we

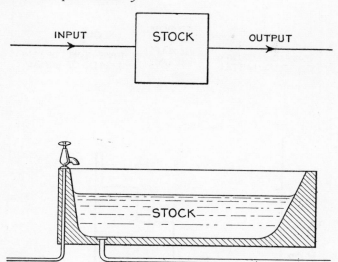

FIG 2 *Basic Stock Centre*

usually want to do is isolate or 'uncouple' two processes from each other. Our second example shows this; let us suppose that we are producing a ton of scrap metal every day and removing it in five-ton loads; then we shall need to accumulate a stock. We are no longer interested in the stock for its own sake, but must have it in order to uncouple the output process (remove scrap in five-ton loads) from the input process (receive scrap in daily one-ton lots). The typical pattern of the stock of scrap metal is shown in Fig. 3 on the following page.

Now look at some wider aspects of this 'uncoupling' purpose, by considering a third example. A hydro-electric plant accumulates water in a lake or reservoir, from which water is drawn off to the generators. The rainfall, which is the input, follows a yearly seasonal trend; the water needed at the generators follows a more complicated daily-cum-yearly pattern of demand for electricity. The stock of water contained in the reservoir enables the generators to fulfil the demand in almost complete independence of the rainfall. Almost complete, but not quite. Although we are able to predict the average rainfall—say sixty inches—over several years within close limits, in any one year it may lie anywhere between forty and ninety inches. A succession of dry years would affect the demand by

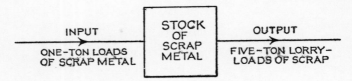

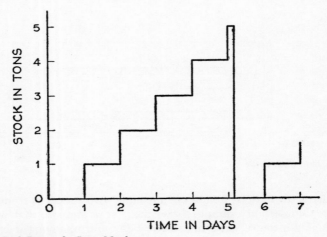

Fig 3 *Stock Pattern for Scrap Metal*

making it necessary to ration the supply. Here we have introduced the idea of an input process which varies in quantity in an unpredictable way. It is not entirely unpredictable though, because we know its average value and the limits within which it will probably fall. The theory of probability can help us in such cases, and does in fact play a large part in modern methods of setting stock levels.

Systems which do not immediately appear to have anything to do with stock control can often be expressed in terms of input-stock-output and the same general theories will apply. The petty cash box resembles the scrap-metal example in reverse—the output trickles away while the input comes in in chunks. An Aga cooker accumulates a 'stock' of heat at a steady rate, holds it in a massive iron casting and releases it according to a fluctuating demand which follows a day and night pattern, its stock absorbing a variation in the demand for energy, not materials.

Stocks may uncouple other types of process which do not concern quantities of material. When successive batches from a chemical process are blended to obtain a more regular quality, they accumulate as a 'quality buffer stock'. Its size will depend upon the required specification as the output and the natural variation of the process as the input.

So-called 'speculative stocks' uncouple a selling process from a buying process; the speculator manipulates his stock of a commodity so as to make the greatest profit from variations in price. An entirely opposite motive lies behind the buffer stock of tin operated by the International Tin Council, for whereas the private speculator welcomes wide ranges of price, the Council aims at stabilizing prices. If the price of tin goes too high, the Buffer Stock Manager brings it down by selling tin from stock, and vice versa. In 1951, five years before the stock was created, the Korean war caused tin prices to vary between £805 and £1,620 per ton; in 1956 the range had fallen to £167 (in spite of the Suez crisis) and in 1959 it was only £55. The buffer stock continued to fulfil its purpose until June, 1961, when all 10,000 tons of it were sold in a vain attempt to hold the price of tin at £880 in the face of a predicted world-wide shortage.

We may also mention in passing the *strategic* stocks of raw materials such as tungsten, which uncouple the demands of a country from the privations of war.

As a final example, we have a description of a stock which serves all three purposes—uncoupling of quantity, quality, and price; it is taken from one of Cyril Ray's articles on wine in *The Observer*—

> . . . the price of sherry does not vary from year to year as that of table wine does. This is because sherry is made on the *solera* system, by adding younger to older wines, over the years, so that price, as well as style and quality, is kept steady—it would need a number of bad years running before the price of a bottle of sherry in a London wine merchants reflected the fact that a thousand miles away moth and rust had corrupted the grapes it came from . . . . Similarly, the system can absorb a small drop in production or a rise in price: it has to be a very big pinch for a firm with a million gallons of sherry in its *bodega* to feel it.

We can see from this selection of examples that a single principle—uncoupling—lies at the heart of all stock control and has a very wide range of applications.

One of the most interesting analogues of a stock control system is the suspension of a motor-car. Here the input is 'shocks caused by uneven road surfaces' and the output is 'shocks transmitted to the passengers' (Fig. 4). The suspension contains three main elements: tyres, road springs, and seat cushions, and its object is to 'uncouple'

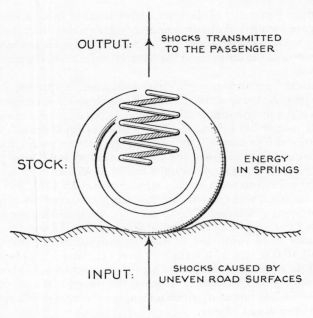

OUTPUT: SHOCKS TRANSMITTED
TO THE PASSENGER

STOCK: ENERGY
IN SPRINGS

INPUT: SHOCKS CAUSED BY
UNEVEN ROAD SURFACES

FIG 4 *Stock Analogy: Suspension of a Motor-car*

the passenger completely from the road surface. It is this useful parallel which has led us to adopt the phrase 'buffer stock' for a stock which absorbs random or unpredictable disturbances.

The perfect suspension system is unknown; no matter how carefully the springs are designed, the passengers will still feel the effects of two potholes a wheelbase-length apart, or other relatively rare irregularities. The designer must balance the various factors such as cost and availability of materials, steering, rolling and pitching tendencies, to achieve what he considers a reasonable compromise. In the same way, the buffer stock will never succeed in completely uncoupling one process from another. We need to consider the cost of the stock itself, of housing, heating, handling and recording it, and so on. Like the motor-car designer, we must aim at a reasonable compromise which falls short of the ideal. The problem lies in deciding what we mean by 'reasonable'.

Have you ever driven a motor-car in which the shock absorbers have failed? If so, you will know that within a certain range of speed the vehicle is afflicted with 'judder', a rapid but regular vibration of the whole body. This is because the road springs, like a tuning fork, have a natural period of vibration in these conditions. The designer counters this by adding the so-called 'shock absorbers' (more correctly called 'dampers') to damp down this natural vibration. An exactly similar phenomenon can occur in stock units for they may in certain conditions begin to oscillate wildly up and down, and we can oppose this tendency just as the car designer does —by adding a 'damper'. The damper in our case will be an arithmetical one rather than an assembly of metal and rubber, but both devices share the same principle.

Let us now take the analogy further, and think about the shape of the road surface. What exactly is a 'bump' or a 'pothole'? When does a large bump become a small hill? You can see the parallel between the last question and 'When does a rise in sales cease to be a large temporary fluctuation and become the beginning of an upward trend?' Simple statistical methods can help us to answer questions like this, as we shall see. But here a word of caution—they can only help for there is no complete substitute for decisions.

Making decisions is the essence of management, and a managerial decision may well be defined as 'selecting a preferred course of action from several alternatives when the available information is inadequate'. In the face of inadequate information, that mysterious attribute variously called administrative skill, judgment or 'hunch' must be invoked. No-one knows how the brain arrives at a conclusion in such circumstances, but it does, in some way we cannot (yet) fathom. It follows, therefore, that we cannot reduce decision-taking to a complete and all-embracing set of rules; so we cannot delegate the control in its entirety. The aim of the management scientist is to reduce as much as possible of the decision process to routine and in the pages which follow we shall see the extent to which he has succeeded. It is heartening to remember that even a superficial understanding of the methods he has devised can lead to a less cluttered life for the senior manager because more and more of an organization's trivia will be cleared from his desk leaving space for him to concentrate on the exercise of his judgment. The decisions he takes will become of greater moment, as we shall see in Chapter 10, but for this very reason they will enhance the satisfaction conveyed by a good job well done.

What bedevils the manager is often the sheer *complexity* of the system he must control. The methods described here will help to reduce complex systems to their simpler elements. Greater finesse in the analysis can lead to greater delicacy in control.

In illustration of this, consider Fig. 1 as representing only the first stage of an analysis. We could make it more detailed by including, say, the 'stock' of caustic soda solution held in the pipes. Such minute detail would be an absurdity here, but pipe-line stocks may be considerable in the oil industry—every mile of a 24-inch pipe holds 400 tons of oil.

In general, we can make our picture or 'model' of the stock system as complicated or as simple as we like. If we make it very complicated, we get a good approximation to reality but may find it too cumbersome to handle conveniently. A simple version would be cheaper and easier to handle but less realistic.

> Then must we rate the cost of the erection;
> Which if we find outweighs ability,
> What do we then but draw anew the model
> In fewer offices . . . ?

From Shakespeare we descend to the jargon of technicians in this field, to find that the concept of a 'model' is freely used. They use the word in exactly the same sense as Shakespeare: a simplified representation of reality, convenient for planning.

Although there are other types of stock, in general it is a stock of *goods* which is most important to the business man. The input feeds into that stock, the output is drawn out of it and the stock itself serves the purpose of making these two flows to some extent (though not entirely) independent of each other. Thus stock control depends on linking the output to the input through an *informational* link rather than a *material* one. The use of *material* to transmit *messages* is one of the most fundamental causes of excessive stocks. So the modern revolution in inventory control rests on the use of information as a means of regulation rather than direct control with the materials themselves. In the modern jargon, we talk about an 'informational model' of the stocks. This model is, as we have said, a *simplified* description of the physical components of the stock system; it may take the form of an accounting ledger, a battery of charts, a set of mathematical equations, a pack of punched cards, or even the electrical and magnetic impulses in an electronic computer.

Models are used so widely, especially in matters of money, that we tend to lose sight of their abstract nature and confuse them with reality. Think of your own bank account—is it a model? It is, and even the money in your pocket, apparently so much more tangible than a bank statement, is a representation of some other 'reality'. Fortunately for us, the 'reality' of our stock systems is much more obvious than that of pure economics.

So we have the reality—the physical stocks—and the model which is presented to the executive. What is it that links them?

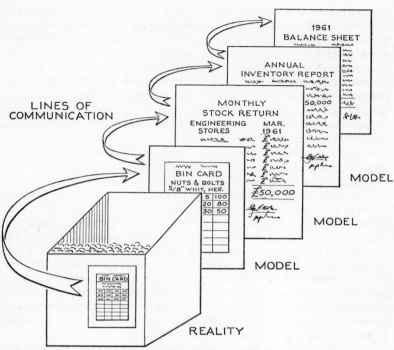

FIG 5 *Lines of Communication from Physical Stocks to Models*

Surely it is the lines of communication (Fig. 5). Suppose we have a real stock of fifty dozen nuts and bolts in a bin. The storekeeper counts or weighs them; he enters their quantity and description on a bin card and then periodically on a form for the return of stock— 'Bolts and Nuts, M.S. Whitworth, $2'' \times \frac{5}{8}''$ dia. hexagon, 50 doz.'— This is sent to the stock controller or accountant, and may appear as part of the item 'Miscellaneous Engineering Stores, £50,000' and eventually in an even more simplified model, the 'Total Inventory' in the annual balance sheet. Here we have a line of communication which consists of the storekeeper, the accountant, and the forms they use. It connects the physical stocks not merely to one model, but to several. Moreover it is obviously only one of a widespread network of communications and it is this network, together with the physical stocks themselves, which make up what we have called the 'stock system'.

Two types of specialists concern themselves with the study of these communications networks. We may say broadly that the Organization and Methods experts are responsible for the general layout of the network, whereas the accountants are concerned with the messages which flow along them. The two functions are combined in the new specialism called Systems Engineering.

One cannot help but compare such systems with the muscles of the body and the nerves which connect them to their controller, the brain.

As we saw in Fig. 1, stocks may be classified by the nature of the input and output uncoupled from each other. If the input is material that you are buying in from some outside source and the output is your first manufacturing stage then, of course, your stock is of *raw materials*. If your input and output are two successive stages of manufacture your stock is *work in progress*. If your input is the finished result of your manufacture and the output is sales to customers then, of course, your stock item is a *finished product*. These are the three main headings under which stock tends to be accumulated for inventory-taking. Accountants and other experts have been known to argue quite fiercely amongst themselves about what constitutes one's inventory. Some will maintain with great force that it is only finished products and others will say only finished products and raw materials ('but not your work in progress—that isn't inventory, that is work in progress!') The only logical approach is to take all three types as being components of total inventory.

Uncoupling which is the purpose of any stock centre, renders one process to some extent independent of another. The evolution of stock control theory along modern lines has followed the development of this statement. The uncoupling is what you want to achieve. It is the *benefit* you get from stock. A stock buys time—*time* to cover delays in the delivery of raw materials; *time* to take advantage of when scheduling production in the most efficient way; or time that manifests itself in the speed with which finished goods are delivered to customers.

Herein lies a parallel to the reaction time in a human being. How quickly do you pull your fingers back from a hot surface? How quickly can your organization react to a demand made upon it? (This question confines our thinking to finished goods and it is with this class of stock most of the classical work has been done.) In general one wants to be able to supply a customer quickly, to give virtually instantaneous service. In examining inventory policy for finished goods, look at your terms of sale. These are very interesting to investigate in any company because often you will see in the publicity material that the company undertakes to fulfil any order within, say, 48 hours of its receipt. It is then wise to heed the advice of Francis Bacon who said "We should be grateful to Machiavel and others who tell us what men are wont to do and not what men ought to do". If you look at the procedure which is *actually* adopted in dealing with orders, you will find very often an enthusiastic sales manager insisting that a newly-received order be got out on the same day by a costly method in spite of the terms as formally stated. You will also find that the level of service being given is often above that promised and therefore most probably better than that being paid for by the customer.

One large oil company calculated the benefits of speeding up the invoicing of bunkerage, that is refuelling ships at sea and in port. It was found that a speed-up of one day represented an effective saving of one million pounds of capital. This shows that you cannot divorce stock control from things like office procedure, financial policy and so on, they are all part of the intertwining total system. It also shows one way of making a start on stock policy. Dictate what your 'reaction time' is to be, that is, how quickly you will supply a customer's order and how quickly *he* must react to this service by paying you for it. Until he does, he is your debtor, and it is no coincidence that 'Stocks and Debtors' so often appear as a single item in a balance sheet. This, of course, refers in the main to one particular section of manufacturing industry, the section which deals with mass-produced (or at best batch-produced) goods. (Although there are cases in which stock control tends to be dominated by considerations of production, in consumer goods it tends to be the other way round.) Now an accumulation of excessive stock means in practical terms a delay in payment for what you have done. You have bought raw materials, applied your productive resources to them, and produced some kind of end-product; your next concern is to get the money flowing in from the customer. If you are not paid soon for that finished material now held immobile in stock you will deprive yourself of that monetary inflow, and that deprivation is your main cost in holding excessive stocks. You can separate the cost of stocks into two components—financial and physical. This simple division is discussed in more detail in Chapter 10, it suffices for the moment to note that the former predominates and will force you to put some sort of valuation on capital. To ascertain this we can ask either of two questions—

(*a*) What does it cost to borrow the capital? *or*
(*b*) What would it earn if we put it into something else? (This is sometimes referred to as the opportunity cost.)

Which of these you adopt is one aspect of setting the policy in your business for this is the kind of decision that you must take if you bear the responsibility for inventory policy, and it is the kind of decision the answer to which you cannot just go and look up in a textbook.

It is rather like playing a hand of bridge if you reach a point when you want to finesse a king and you decide to 'take a view'. You play as though the king were, perhaps, on your left hand but the important thing is to play *consistently* in accordance with your 'view'. If you play one trick as though the king were on your left hand and the next trick as though it were on your right hand, you are almost certain to lose your finesse. Similarly but much more importantly, you should take a consistent view of the cost of capital tied up in stocks. In deciding this item of your business policy, you should review in your mind all possible ways in which you could put your available capital to work. Consider the whole range of alternatives, including the practice of keeping large amounts of money locked up in investment in other companies. Many people may consider this prudence, to others it is a confession of failure: one would be justified in saying to the Board of that company, "I have entrusted you with some of my money in order that you may put it to work and earn some more money for me. Now you appear to think that part of that money can be handled by some other group in whose resources you have invested it. Why, then, should I not simply take my money back from you and invest it in that other group myself directly, especially since you have done nothing very much to convince me of your abilities as managers of money anyway?" Investment elsewhere is one possible outlet for your money, but there are others. For example, there may be opportunities for acquiring new plant, new productive resources of other sorts or buildings to house them. In such a case one very often finds an inconsistency in policy. In one company a proposal connected with storage which showed a pay-back in two years was turned down on the grounds that the company just could not afford the policy. They said "Why, yes, the figures are quite convincing and if we had the capital we would certainly put it in, but we haven't, you see, so that represents an absolute bar." This meant that by implication they were valuing their capital at 50% per annum. Hence it is valuable, in a variety of industries, to look closely at the *consistency* of your company's capital investment policy, especially since a heavy investment in stock is often associated with a bank overdraft—and what is a bank overdraft but a kind of negative investment? Some items of a company's operations may not on the face of it appear to have anything to do with inventory control, but in the light of this approach, *consistency* in investment policy, they may well turn out to be very relevant indeed to total policy. You must assess the benefits which you wish to accrue to you from every item of your stock.

One of the main purposes in having stock in olden days was ostentation—a bulging granary and/or a fat wife showed the world that you were prosperous! That reason has almost entirely disappeared, for like personal protuberance, corporate corpulence is no longer fashionable.

Sometimes nowadays one has to deal with a company or department of a company which is in business purely to deal in stock as a wholesaler. Steel stockholders are such, and they claim to offer a useful service in that they hold a variety of types of steel and can supply these very quickly. The position of steel stockholders as operating companies is a most interesting one, because they are not pure stockholders at all. They do, in fact, process their stock in that they cut it to size, and that is about all they do do, apart from handling. But the 'purity' of merely *holding* the stock, taking orders from a customer and replenishing from a supplier is somewhat dimmed by the fact that processing *is* done upon it. Consider also stocks of champagne undergoing the second or 'malo-lactic' ferment, and stocks of whisky ("Not a drop is sold 'til it's seven years old"). Are these, in fact, stocks which uncouple one process from another or are they stocks of work in progress in that chemical reactions are still going on in them? So in scientific inventory control, as in the application of any management technique which will in general be mathematical or statistical, you are forced to make decisions or assumptions about the exact nature of your business and what is going on in it. Sometimes it is very easy to check these assumptions and yet not everyone bothers to do so. Sometimes, though, it can be very difficult indeed.

To sum up, then, two key factors in stock control are the *benefit* you get from the stock in terms of time and the capital and revenue *costs* incurred in holding it. Stock control is therefore an example of *cost-benefit analysis*. An analogy has already been drawn with the brain. What we shall discuss in the chapters which follow is the 'brain' which controls the system—the models which the executive considers and the decisions which he applies to them.

Having looked briefly at the complex systems which can be built up from the basic unit, let us go back to that unit and study it in rather more detail. How exactly do we define which materials belong to a stock and which do not? Can we include in our finished stock goods which have not been formally inspected and passed, if in our experience they are practically certain to be approved? Obviously, we must begin by deciding where to put the 'stock boundaries': the input boundary is the point at which materials cease to be involved in the 'input' process and the output boundary is that at which they begin to take part in the 'output' process. It takes a man with a good knowledge of the manufacturing processes to say exactly where these boundaries ought to be. In fact, this question of defining stock can be so hard to deal with in practice that I have chosen to discuss it as a practical example in Appendix 1. This example shows how we may have to set boundaries in different places for different types of control; it also shows once again how we need to look at whole sets of operations rather than odd bits here and there. Appendix I uses one of the methods of Work Study—flow process charting—and also shows how the method of systematic questioning can be applied to stocks. A good background of Work Study can be a great help in the practical application of stock control; one of the best of the many books available is that by Alan Fields (*see* footnote on page 156).

A stock system now begins to appear as something which permeates a whole organization, whether the organization be for manufacturing, distributing, buying and selling, or all of these together. Each individual stock centre serves to uncouple two or more processes from each other, but what does the stock system as a whole achieve? We can look upon it as a lubricant which allows the whole set of processes to run smoothly; individual stock centres between processes are like oil films between surfaces, allowing one surface (or process) to move smoothly and independently of the other. Or better still, let us think of the stock system as a *machine* which lubricates the whole organization. This may appear to be a rather startling idea. Why, in any case, should we use this particular concept? Because we are still aiming at the idea of *control*, and control demands a knowledge of *performance*. We must set a standard of performance and then control the system so that this standard is maintained.

If you feel reluctant to accept the idea of a stock 'machine', pause for a moment to decide exactly what the word 'machine' means to you (for example, is a chimney a machine?), and then look at the following description of a stock system—

(1) It is made up of physical parts whose cost is known; capital is invested in it and has to be justified by some return.

(2) It has to be housed, maintained and regularly inspected: it needs a good deal of skilled attention.

(3) It performs a definite service to the organization, which could not function without it.

Think of your own stock system or 'machine'. Does it fit this description? If so, it may be a sobering experience to ask yourself three questions about it—

First: How much of your capital is invested in it?

Second: How much skill, experience and discussion were devoted to the design and specification of the stock machine, when compared with a similar investment in, say, new machine tools?

Third: How much skill, experience and money are devoted to the operation, maintenance and development of the stock machine, compared with other machines of similar value elsewhere in your company?

All three questions ask "How much are you putting in?" and the first one, at least, can be answered precisely. One must also ask "What return are you getting out?" and so far the answer is a vague one—'lubrication' or 'smooth running'. We shall tackle this problem of return: meanwhile, let it be assumed that we are able to find a way of measuring the economic return of a stock machine.

Then, and not before, can we begin to control it. We can prescribe that return which we expect from our known investment and running costs and we can install the means of attaining and retaining that output. This is true stock control—a control which takes in the stock system as a *whole*, set in the whole organization. Only this overall approach can give us a firm foundation for erecting our control structure; only this unified concept can enable us to review the individual stock items in a balanced and consistent way.

Stock Control is something which enables us to make the best use of one particular resource, the stock system. Just what we mean by 'the best use' is still a matter for some debate, but widely accepted interpretation is 'minimizing total costs'. The next chapter illustrates the way in which this principle is translated into practice.

Many companies are proud of their non-existent stock control system: non-existent, because their so-called system lacks the essential core—a target or objective which is to be achieved—and so remains a mere stock recording system, a nervous system without a guiding brain. True stock control—

(1) maps out the stock system,

(2) balances the cost of holding stocks against the advantages which they confer

(3) so as to define a set of target stocks which minimize total costs; it also

2

(4) provides the means for bringing the system to the target state and

(5) the means for revising the targets in the light of changing conditions.

CHAPTER 2

Economic Lot Sizes

Some have too much, yet still do crave;
I little have, and seek no more.
They are but poor, though much they have,
And I am rich with little store.

SIR EDWARD DYER, *My Mind to Me a Kingdom Is.*

The problem of economic lot sizes provides a simple illustration of the way in which we apply the principle of balancing one cost against another so as to keep our total cost to a minimum. Let us begin by considering a simple imaginary example. You are running a warehouse, buying in bulk and selling in small quantities. One of the commodities with which you deal is a chemical called chocolic acid: you buy it at five shillings a ton and sell it at a steady rate of one hundred tons a week. The maker will supply it to you in multiples of one ton; he is exceptionally reliable and always delivers on time. You have to decide how much to order at a time.

The output, then, is a steady flow of 100 tons a week. We are going to try and find out what the input should be, knowing that it will come in in batches. Let us for the time being assume the simplest possible case—that we order one week's supply at a time. Then each batch or *lot* will contain 100 tons. The administrative (and other) costs associated with a single order come to 96p (£0·96) whatever its size, so they will take £0·96 per week. This is shown by the first entry in the column headed 'Ordering Cost' in Table I on page 20.

Note that the units in which we have decided to work are tons, weeks and pounds sterling. It is important to keep consistently to whatever units are chosen, otherwise the arithmetic can go wrong in a confused tangle of tons per week, per cent per annum, pence per order and price per pound or kilogramme.

Fig. 6 shows the stock pattern generated by the input-output process as we have described it so far. In this simple pattern, we can see that the average stock is equal to half the batch size, so for

TABLE I: *Costs of ordering and stockholding for chocolic acid in £ sterling per week (Sales 100 tons per week)*

Lot Size (tons)	Ordering Cost £/week	Stockholding Cost £/week	Total Cost £/week
100	0·96	0·06	1·02
200	0·48	0·12	0·60
300	0·32	0·18	0·50
400*	0·24	0·24	0·48
500	0·19	0·30	0·49
600	0·16	0·36	0·52

* Economic Lot Size.

hundred-ton batches we shall hold, on the average, 50 tons of chocolic acid in stock.

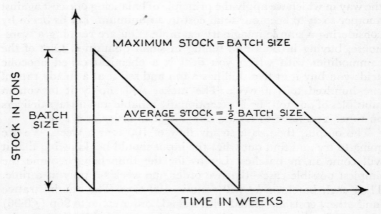

FIG 6 *Stock Pattern for Chocolic Acid*

The value of this stock at £0·24 per ton, is £12·00. We now suppose that the capital tied up in it is worth 25% per annum—in round figures this is ½% per week and ½% of £12·00 is £0·06 (six new pence). This amount is found in Table I as the first entry under 'Stockholding Cost', and when added to the Ordering Cost (£0·96) it gives a total weekly cost of £1·02. This total cost is the one we may change by altering the lot size and thereby the stock.

Suppose we act without thinking and say "Get the stocks *down*! Halve the lot size!". Then the new 50-ton lot will give us an average stock of 25 tons, value £6·00 and thus costing £0·03 a week. But we are ordering twice as frequently, so the ordering cost has doubled, reaching £1·92 a week. Our reduction in stock, then, has been dearly bought, for our total weekly cost will have gone up from £1·02 to £1·95.

It obviously does not always pay to reduce stock levels—indeed, in this simple case the stock has been brought *too* low. So let us now think of doubling the lot size instead of halving it. For a 200-ton order the average stock will be 100 tons, value £24·00, weekly cost (at ½ per cent) £0·12. Orders are placed (and lots arrive) every two weeks; the weekly ordering cost is now only £0·48, giving a new total of £0·60 as the second line of entries in Table I shows.

Our figures confirm that it will pay us to increase the stock, that is, the batch size, but common sense tells us that this cannot go on indefinitely. Table I gives the costs for even bigger batches and shows that the smallest total cost, £0·48 per week, corresponds to a lot size of 400 tons. This we call the *optimum* lot size or *economic* lot size.

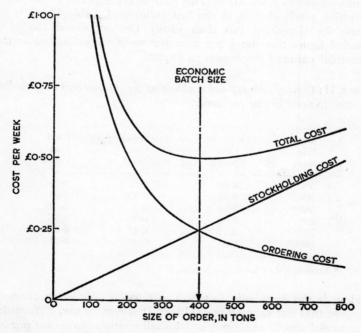

Fig 7 *Economic Lot Size: Table I in Graphical Form*

'Optimum' is a technical term much in favour amongst management scientists: it means 'maximum or minimum, whichever is appropriate' and since we are discussing costs rather than profits, the optimum batch is the one which has the minimum total cost associated with it.

Fig. 7 shows Table I in graphical form. In it, one can see that the stockholding cost increases in direct proportion to the lot size: every hundred tons we add to the batch size adds 50 tons to the stock and £0·06 to its weekly cost in terms of working capital.

The ordering cost, however, decreases *hyperbolically* as shown by the curved line (hyperbola) in Fig. 7. The total cost, which is the sum of the two, reaches a minimum at the point where the two costs are equal, which is where the slope of the 'ordering cost' curve is exactly the same as the slope of the stockholding cost curve apart from being downwards instead of upwards. At this point, in the jargon of the economist, 'marginal benefit equals marginal cost'.

The curve of total cost has a very flat minimum, which shows us that the economic lot size is not very sensitive to small errors in the figures we use to calculate it. This flatness corresponds to the three successive totals of 0·68 in the last column of Table II; it is no excuse for sloppiness but does justify the occasional use of a rounded figure like the ½ per cent per week we estimated as the numerical value of the return on capital.

TABLE II: *Costs of ordering and stockholding for chocolic acid in £ sterling per week (Sales 200 tons per week)*

Lot Size (tons)	Ordering Cost £/week	Stockholding Cost £/week	Total Cost £/week
400	0·48	0·24	0·72
500	0·38	0·30	0·68
566*	0·34	0·34	0·68
600	0·32	0·36	0·68
700	0·27	0·42	0·69
800	0·24	0·48	0·72

* Economic Lot Size.

How is the Economic Lot Size affected if conditions change? Suppose that our sales were doubled? It is easy to say, "We order four weeks' supply at a time, so we shall continue to do so: our lot size will be 800 tons." Easy, yes, but also wrong. Our average stock is still half the lot size, so the stockholding cost increases in proportion to the amount ordered. However, the saving in ordering costs gets progressively less as we increase the amount ordered. Table II shows the new conditions.

The ordering and stockholding costs are equal (apart from rounding-off fractions) at 566 tons, and it is this quantity, not 800 tons, which is the new economic lot size. This example shows how a too-simple re-ordering rule may lead one astray. It also shows the effect of not adjusting one's rules to suit new conditions. If we had kept to 400 tons as the ordering quantity and congratulated ourselves that costs per ton had fallen because of increased sales, we should have been overlooking the possibility of the even greater saving associated with 566-ton orders. On the other hand, the rule "Order four weeks' supply" would also have been uneconomic.

We can calculate the economic lot size directly from the four figures which we used as working data. They were—

(1) the rate of sales, 100 tons a week;
(2) the cost of chocolic acid, £0·24 a ton;
(3) the return required on capital, 26 per cent per year ($\frac{1}{2}$ per cent per week);
(4) the cost of placing an order, £0·96.

First we make sure that all four factors are expressed in the right units. If the sales are in tons *per week*, then the rate of return on capital must be per cent *per week* also, not per year. The value of the material must be in pounds sterling per *ton*, or new pence per ton; if it is in pence then the cost of ordering must also be in pence.

Then to find the economic lot size—

(1) Multiply the rate of sales by the ordering cost.
(2) Multiply the cost per item by the rate of return (as a percentage).
(3) Divide the first answer by the second.
(4) Multiply by 200.
(5) Take the square root.

If we take the data provided in Table II as an example, we have the following calculation—

(1)	200 tons per week × £0·96	= 192
(2)	£0·24 per ton × $\frac{1}{2}$ per cent per week	= 0·12
(3)	192 ÷ 0·12	= 1,600
(4)	1,600 × 200	= 320,000
(5)	Square Root of 320,000	= 566

and since the original units were tons, the answer is also in tons.

When we use this method of finding the economic lot size, we find that the lot size varies in proportion to the square root of the sales. In the example quoted, sales were supposed to have increased by a factor of 2. The factor for multiplying the lot size is 1·414 which is the square root of 2; 400 multiplied by this factor gives, to the nearest ton, a lot size of 566 tons.

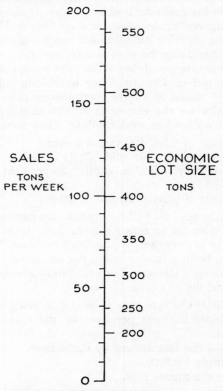

Fig 8 *How Economic Lot Size Varies with Sales*

When all the other factors are constant, as is often the case, the relationship between the rate of sales and the economic lot size can be expressed as a double scale as shown in Fig. 8. This device can be used to obtain the economic lot size directly from a chart showing the trend of sales with the passage of time. (*See* Fig. 33, page 24.)

It is worth our while to examine the method of calculation in some detail, because it can be used to show some important principles as well as to demonstrate the fallacies which can arise in applying it. We have already seen that the economic lot size is proportional to the square root of the rate of sales. How do other factors affect it?

If the cost of the material goes up, the amount of capital invested in stock also increases, and so does the stockholding cost: the economic lot size will therefore become smaller. We can show, by methods similar to those used in investigating changes in sales, that if the cost were to double, the lot size would need to be *divided* by the square root of 2. In fact, all the relationships between the economic lot size and the factors from which we calculate it contain this square root element. For this reason it is known as 'the square root law', and was one of the very first principles of stock control to be discovered. An early paper by Camp on this subject was written in 1922, and the formula has been faithfully copied from one textbook to another and applied with varying degrees of skill ever since. You can usually apply it to individual orders from outside suppliers, but attempts to use it for drawing up internal production schedules may end in disaster, as I shall show later.

Continuing our investigation of the individual factors, let us look now at the return on capital. The rate of sales and the unit cost are peculiar to individual items of stock, but the rate of return and cost of ordering are universal factors within the same firm. The cost of ordering is not a controllable factor, but the rate of return is: it is a *policy* figure set by you, the executive. As such it can be a most powerful weapon of control, as we shall see in more detail later (Chapter 10). The effect of varying it is the same as that of varying the unit cost: if we multiply the rate of return by some number, we must divide the economic lot size by the square root of the same number. Table III shows how the average capital investment in stock can be controlled by setting the rate of return at different levels.

TABLE III: *Effect of rate of return on capital invested in stock* (*Chocolic acid, 100 tons per week*)

Required Rate of Return % per year	Economic Lot Size tons	Capital Invested in Stock £ (average)
6%	800	£96
12%	566	£68
25%	400	£48
50%	283	£34

In Table III the rule about consistent units has been broken

2*

deliberately, capital costs having been put in per cent per annum simply because in this form they are more familiar to the company executive. This table is meant to help him see how a policy imposed in quantitative form can have a positive effect on stock levels. Of course, it is not easy to decide what the figure shall be. Although Bank Rate is always a good guide, especially if the company has an overdraft, it is only one aspect of the cost of borrowing in general, and debentures issued by the company, if any, are almost bound to affect the level at which the company's own rate is set. So, in these days of inflation, is the natural desire to hold one's assets in the form of goods rather than as a paper credit provided, of course, that the goods are not perishable nor obsolescent.

Also, alternative opportunities for internal investment must not be overlooked. There is no golden rule for setting this important figure, for ultimately it can only be a matter of your judgment; it is, so to speak, a throttle control for your stock machine. Here, surely, is one of the answers to those who fear that scientific methods tend to take skill and experience out of management, substituting the moronic operation of rigid mathematical laws. Quite the reverse—such scientific methods as this one concentrate and amplify your managerial skill, in making one policy decision effective over an entire range of stocks and sales.

Finally, let us descend to a more parochial level and consider the cost of ordering, about which there has been some loose thinking in the past. If we place just one extra order, do we in fact spend just one extra pound? Or if we place one order less, do we save a pound? The answer to both these questions could be yes—our staff may be working overtime costing £1 per order, which can be increased or decreased within certain limits.

Similarly, you may have a large organization which employs casual labour in the Buying Department, or in which the total staff can be increased or decreased fairly readily. These possibilities by no means cover all the cases, for the greater part of British industry is still concentrated in small companies which are likely to have relatively small buying offices. If such an office can handle, say, 5,000 orders a year, then our problem will be to allocate this number of orders to all the material items so as to minimize costs. Subtracting a few odd orders may increase the typists' output of knitting but will make no difference to the cost of running the office. The *total* ordering costs will be constant, so we should try to make the *total* stockholding cost as low as possible by placing the greatest possible number of orders with the most economical allocation. A method for doing this is given in Appendix 2.

We have, of course, assumed rather glibly that we know the cost of ordering or the total capacity of our existing buying office. It is more likely that we do not, and we shall have to find out these figures with the help of the cost accountant and the Work Study or O. & M. people. Here we can see again how one branch of scientific management impinges on another and how the various techniques help each other.

At the risk of being accused of sacrilege, one might also say that, in the early stages at least, a shrewd guess at the ordering cost can be a great help, especially if it is dignified by the name of 'estimate.'

Still considering the small buying department, we should not rule out the possibility of increasing or decreasing the total staff so as to achieve a net saving. We then have to balance the extra cost of the buying staff against the reduction in stockholding cost which can be obtained from the best allocation of the greater capacity for placing orders; the point to bear in mind is that our ordering capacity will be increased stepwise by quite a large proportion—say 20 per cent. An example of this type is also given in Appendix 2.

Next, a word about discounts. So far, we have assumed the cost of an item to be independent of the quantity ordered; often this is not true. A quantity discount or discounts will come into effect at some fixed level or levels of ordering: this will make it necessary to calculate the economic lot size twice—with and without the discount—and then choose the cheaper. Appendix 3 gives an example of this.

Seasonal discounts ("It's cheaper to buy *now!*") are subject to exactly the same fundamental principle of minimizing total cost. If we buy more than we need now, we get the excess at a cheaper price, *but* we hold it in stock for several months, tie up the equivalent capital and incur stockholding costs which must be balanced against the saving in price. Such discounts are offered for household coal, which is, say, £20 a ton in winter and £19 in summer. If we order a ton in June for use in December, we tie up £19 for six months. This £19 invested in the Post Office Savings Bank would earn about 25 new pence in six months; it is worth sacrificing this to save a pound. We have assumed that storage costs us nothing, but a keen gardener might look at the area covered by coal and wish to add a 'cost of lost vegetables' to the loss of interest.

These principles are not new and it would be an insult to a competent buyer to suggest that he was not already aware of them, *as principles*. What *is* new is their assessment in terms of actual figures; this has probably not been done before in your business because some of the required figures are difficult to define—in particular, the return on capital. Nevertheless, their evaluation is well worth the trouble, for it will free the buyer from the hampering need to make a series of *ad hoc* personal decisions. A few rulings on policy will enable his subordinates to deal with these cases as a matter of routine; the buyer will be free to devote himself to those intricate parts of his work in which there is no substitute for human judgment.

The Optimum Number of Orders

Closely allied to the idea of the Economic Lot Size is that of the Optimum Number of Orders (ONO), which in some ways is more convenient.

We found the ELS for chocolic acid to be 400 tons when the sales were 100 tons a week. We can express this in a different way by saying that the *optimum frequency* of ordering is once every four weeks; the Optimum Number of Orders per week is 100/400, i.e. 0·25, i.e. 13 orders a year.

We calculated this useful figure by dividing the batch size into the rate of sales, but it may be arrived at more directly in the following way—

(1) Multiply the cost of an order by 200.

(2) Divide the rate of return on capital by the result from step (1).

(3) Take the square root of the quotient from step (2); call it the *constant*.

(4) Multiply the rate of sales by the cost per item to get the value of sales; call this the *turnover* (although this term, though commonly used and understood, is equivocal and should not be confused with the rate of turnover of stock (*see* page 100). 'Value of sales' is less convenient but has the merit of being unambiguous.

(5) Multiply the square root of the turnover by the constant.

The result is the ONO, as will now be demonstrated with the data from the ELS calculation.

(1) £0·96 × 200 = 192
(2) 0·5 (% per week) ÷ 192 = 0·0026
(3) Square Root of 0·0026 = 0·05 which is the *constant*.
(4) 100 (tons per week) × £0·24 = £24·00 which is the *turnover*.
(5) Square Root of 24 = 5
$$5 \times 0·05 = 0·25$$

This confirms the result already obtained.

It happens that in this case the constant is particularly convenient because multiplying by 0·05 is the same as dividing by 20. This sort of calculation is the basis of such systems as Foster's 'Automatic Control by Turnover' and one called 'Coverage Analysis'. In the latter, statistical sampling of the whole range of an organization's stocks is used and the constant is deduced from the current state of affairs; this avoids the difficulties of determining the cost of an order and of setting a return on capital but only by sacrificing optimization to convenience.

We have now examined every factor in the square-root law for economic lot sizes in minute detail: perhaps you feel that we cannot possibly criticize it any further—but we can. Let us look at this rule in two different situations: first, in ordering our raw materials from outside suppliers; second, in scheduling the production of one of our own manufacturing plants.

If we place a group of orders outside, they will not normally affect each other: the delivery of nuts and bolts from Smith & Brown Ltd. will not depend in any way on how much copper tubing we ask Jones & Robinson for. When we have this condition of independence, we can safely use the square-root law. In other words, it is strictly a rule for individual cases.

What happens if we try to apply it to our own production? "After all," you may say, "the Sales Manager places his order with the Production Manager—isn't this the same sort of situation?" Let me show you why it is not.

Imagine that we have an assembly plant which produces washing-machines. The demand for these machines is steady at 600 a month and the capacity of the plant is just equal to this demand. Then there is no question of making washing-machines in batches—we produce them in a continuous stream in step with the sales. There is no *production* stock of finished machines at all, and economic lot sizes do not concern us.

Supposing, though, that our capacity for 600 machines a month coincided with a demand for only 100. Would you sit down to work out economic lot sizes? More probably you would first arrange to occupy your surplus capacity with other assembly jobs—say 200 waste-disposers and 300 refrigerators (assuming the same rate of production for all three types of product).

If you can produce 'in parallel', so that all three types of machine flow through the plant without interruption, then your problems will not include economic lot sizes. They are more likely to be of the type known generically as 'assembly line balancing'. If, however, you have to manufacture 'in series' with washing-machines, waste-disposers, and refrigerators coming out in successive lots, then the question is, "How many of each should we make at a time?" This resembles the ordering problem but with a difference: our three products are not independent of each other, and making extra washing-machines will delay the production of the other two items.

There is another and more serious objection. Suppose that our economic lot sizes, calculated by the square-root law, have the values shown in Table IV. The lot sizes have been corrected for the production rate, as explained in Appendix 4, in which the other details of the three products are given.

See how awkward the consequences are. At the end of the first month's production, our stock of washing-machines will have increased by 10 and that of waste-disposers by 45. The stock of refrigerators, on the other hand, will have gone down by 55. The same thing will happen in the next month, and the next (*see* Fig. 57 in Appendix 4). This is obviously nonsensical: the square-root rule cannot apply in this situation. Our economic lot sizes must be

TABLE IV: *Economic lot sizes for three products in Series (by Square-Root Law)*

Item	Sales per Month	Economic Lot Size
Washing Machines	100	110
Waste Disposers	200	245
Refrigerators	300	245
Total	600	600

directly proportional to the sales for each item. A practical problem of this type and its solution, have been published elsewhere.[1]

Now although we have discarded the law itself in this case, there has been nothing which conflicts with the *principle* behind it—that of minimizing cost. The law is not valid because it applies to orders which we assumed to be quite independent of each other, whereas our three manufactured products are highly *inter*dependent.

We have to consider the whole *cycle* of manufacture; in any one cycle we should make the production of the various items proportional to their rates of sale—in this case, three refrigerators and two

[1] See author's article "Production Control by Electronic Computer", *Chemistry and Industry*, p. 1488 (15th Nov., 1958.)

waste-disposers to every washing-machine. Instead of the cost of ordering, we have the cost of changing over from one product to another.

We can now add up the change-over costs for the whole cycle and balance them against the total stock generated by the cycle so as to obtain the economic cycle time. A calculated example is given in Appendix 4.

There may well be other factors which we should take into account. It takes time as well as money to change over from one product to another: the shorter we make our cycle, the greater the proportion of this unproductive time will be. If we go on shortening the cycle, the productive time may be insufficient to fill the total demand. The change-over costs will then be sharply increased by the consequent loss of profit.

To go into problems of this sort in detail would force us into the mathematics which I have deliberately eschewed and would add nothing to the exposition of general principles of stock control and production control: the close relationship between the two was implied in Chapter 1 when we described the input-output approach to stocks.

We have now looked very closely and critically at the methods used for calculating economic lot sizes. They are a useful and powerful means of control, but they are based on several assumptions which are not always justified. Nothing is more to be deplored than the 'gimmick' approach of using some ready-made formula without first examining its validity. The square-root law is no more a panacea for industrial problems than any other piece of abstract mathematics.

The most important thing is to take the trouble to define your exact problem before setting out to solve it. You will find after doing so that you are already half-way towards a solution which will be far more effective than some hastily-contrived application of a textbook formula.

Exercises

1. Wing-nuts are sold by the gross (144) and cost 10 new pence a gross. It costs 3 new pence to place an order, and the total stockholding cost is 15% per annum. Our requirements of wing-nuts during the coming year are estimated at 75 per month. How many should we order at a time?

2. Calculate the annual costs of ordering and stockholding and check that they are the same.

3. The price of wing-nuts is suddenly increased to 12½ new pence a gross. What is the new economic lot size?

4. With wing-nuts at 12½ new pence a gross, increased expenses in the Buying Department make it likely that the cost of placing an order will be increased. How high would it have to go before we increased the economic lot size to 6 gross?

5. If the cost of an order and the cost of a wing-nut increased simultaneously by 10%, how would the economic lot size be affected?

6. Taking the costs as in Question 1, over what range of demand (in wing-nuts per month) would the lot size remain unchanged?

7. The Shields Storage Company orders six main items, each from a different supplier; the monthly consumption rates and values are given below. The Buying Department has a fixed capacity of 60 orders per month: how should they be allocated so that the value of the total average stock of these six items is as low as possible? What is this value?

Item	Monthly Consumption Rate	Unit Value
Articulators	100	£2·00
Bifurcators	30	5·00
Connectors	10	1·00
Duplicators	40	6·00
Extractors	20	10·00
Filters	200	8·00

8. Garlium oxide is being used at the rate of 1200 tons a year and may be obtained for £3 a ton as long as not less than 100 tons are bought at a time. If you were the Buyer, and it costs 90p to place an order, how many orders a year would you place? (The company policy is to value capital at 20% per annum for stockholding purposes, this figure to include all overheads and not merely financial charges.)

CHAPTER 3

Analysis of Demand and Supply

> The question's very much too wide
> And much too deep, and much too hollow,
> And learned men on either side
> Use arguments I cannot follow.
>
> BELLOC, *Dedicatory Ode.*

The problems which we have attacked so far have one point in common: we have assumed that we know everything about them with absolute certainty. Sales would be exactly one hundred tons in each and every week; replenishments would always arrive dead on time and in exactly the amount ordered. This type of system is called 'deterministic,' because all the figures in it are *determined* precisely. Such a system never exists in real life, but can only be an ideal. Nevertheless, we can sometimes use a deterministic *model* of a real system, as we have done up to now in this book. Any such model must always be an approximate one.

What happens in practice? Weekly sales vary; replenishments are delayed or otherwise unacceptable; stocks deteriorate, perish or go out of fashion. Uncertainty has entered the system and it is no longer deterministic.

In this chapter, we shall look at this new problem of uncertainty and shall assume for the sake of simplicity that only the weekly sales are uncertain; replenishments still arrive in the right amount, undamaged and on time. Instead of a fixed rate of sales of 100 tons a week, we have a more realistic set of figures in Table V, which gives the sales of chocolic acid in each week of 1970. The sales figure has now become what we call a 'stochastic variable'.

The word 'stochastic' is derived from the Greek word for an archer, and with good reason. Just as the archer's arrows group themselves around the 'gold' or bull's-eye of a target, so our weekly sales group themselves around a bull's-eye of 100 tons. The archer, even when he hits the gold, will rarely find his arrow in the exact geometrical centre of the target; it happens that, in the same way, not one of our weekly figures is exactly 100 tons—but eight of them

33

are not more than 5 tons away from it. A reasonably competent
archer will not usually miss the target entirely: only a very
exceptional sales figure would miss a 'target' stretching in this case
from 40 to 160 tons.

In drawing this analogy between the archer's arrows and our own
stochastic sales, we have already begun to see that there are certain
rules governing their variation. These rules are drawn from the
'theory of probability'; we shall consider only the very simplest,
remembering that in the first stages of stock control, general ideas
and principles are more important than mathematical detail.

Let us see if we can find some sort of pattern in the figures of
Table V. The average for the whole year is 98 tons and the
averages for the four separate quarters are—

		Tons
January to March	. . . .	102
April to June	. . . .	93
July to September	. . . .	103
October to December	. . . .	101

TABLE V: *Weekly sales of chocolic acid in tons 1970*

FIRST QUARTER			SECOND QUARTER			THIRD QUARTER			FOURTH QUARTER		
Mth.	Wk.	Sales	Mth.	Wk.	Sales	Mth.	Wk.	Sales	Mth.	Wk.	Sales
	1	89		14	81		27	90		40	131
Jan.	2	60	Apr.	15	84	Jul.	28	84	Oct.	41	124
	3	107		16	87		29	131		42	92
	4	90		17	80		30	119		43	141
	5	108		18	113		31	102		44	70
Feb.	6	103	May	19	114	Aug.	32	124	Nov.	45	113
	7	107		20	103		33	103		46	69
	8	132		21	95		34	55		47	122
	9	109		22	84		35	131		48	88
	10	135		23	89		36	107		49	56
Mar.	11	92	Jun.	24	76	Sep.	37	112	Dec.	50	82
	12	116		25	101		38	86		51	110
	13	80		26	96		39	96		52	110
Total		1,328	Total		1,203	Total		1,340	Total		1,309
Average		102	Average		93	Average		103	Average		101
(Range		75)	(Range		38)	(Range		76)	(Range		85)

Grand Total	5,180
Average for the Year	98
(Overall Range	86)

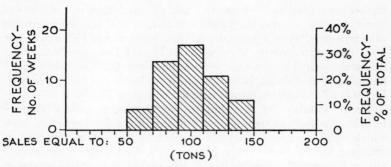

Fɪɢ 9 *Weekly Sales of Chocolic Acid Bar-chart of Frequency Distribution*

There does not seem to be any systematic upward or downward trend here. The low average for the second quarter may perhaps be due to some seasonal effect, but in the absence of any other evidence it is probably no more than a reflection of the general variation.

We can draw a conventional 'bar-chart' or 'histogram' as in Fig. 9 by first grouping the figures into classes or 'slices' of the same range. We count the number of figures in each class and in this way compile the 'frequency distribution' of Table VI.

Tᴀʙʟᴇ VI: *Weekly sales of chocolic acid in 1970: Frequency distribution*

Cʟᴀss Bᴏᴜɴᴅᴀʀɪᴇs			Class Average (tons)	Frequency, i.e. Number in Class	Frequency as Percentage of Total
Lower (tons)		Upper (tons)			
		below 9½	—	0	0
9½	to	29½	19½	0	0
29½	to	49½	39½	0	0
49½	to	69½	59½	4	7·7
69½	to	89½	79½	14	26·9
89½	to	109½	99½	17	32·7
109½	to	129½	119½	11	21·2
129½	to	149½	139½	6	11·5
149½	to	169½	159½	0	0
169½ upwards				0	0
			Total	52	100

This bar-chart is bell-shaped and shows a distribution in which the individual figures cluster about the average value as the arrows cluster around the gold; they become less and less frequent the farther one goes away from the average and they are dispersed symmetrically around it. We do not always find this symmetry in sales figures; they will generally fall into some sort of bell shape, but it is often distorted or 'skewed' as in Fig. 11 (*see* page 36). These frequency distributions can be classified into families, which bear names such as Poisson, Binomial and Log-Normal. Our example in Fig. 9 is of a common family called Normal or Gaussian.

These 'families' of distributions show certain family characteristics, not only in their shapes but also in the mathematical laws which apply to them. They are studied by the statistician, and in drawing up the more refined systems of stock control his expert advice is essential. Nevertheless, at this early stage we can afford to make sweeping assumptions (as long as we do not forget later on just what it was that we *did* assume). For our first crude attack upon stock problems, we shall take it for granted that all our frequency distributions will be as near Normal as makes no matter.

The advantages of this are that the Normal distribution has been found to fit many other sets of figures—the heights of adult males, for example—so it has been closely studied. Statisticians have worked out standard tables which can be applied to any Normal distribution. They have even produced special graph paper for it (of which more presently).

Associated with the idea of 'frequency' is that of 'probability'. About one-third of our weekly sales figures fell into the class ranging between $89\frac{1}{2}$ and $109\frac{1}{2}$ tons; we should expect the same to happen in the sales figures for the following year, unless some change in the customer pattern occurred. This is expressed in the statement, "There is a probability of one-third that any single weekly sales figure for chocolic acid will fall within the range $89\frac{1}{2}$ to $109\frac{1}{2}$ tons."

Although a frequency distribution is built up from a large number of single figures, we can reduce its description to one or two numbers called its 'parameters'. The one which comes immediately to mind is the "average" or "mean": this tells us where the middle of the distribution—the bull's-eye—is. We also need a number—a parameter—which will give us some idea of the *spread* of the distribution. Such a number is the 'range', the difference between the highest and lowest figures; in Table V this is 86 tons, the difference between 141 and 55 tons. It will be evident that one drawback of the range is that it uses only two figures out of the full set, and one of these might easily be freakishly high or low.

A better measure of the spread is the 'standard deviation'. The method of calculating it may be found in any elementary textbook of statistics, but I shall show later how a simple graphical method may be used. The standard deviation for Table V and Fig. 9 is, in fact, 20 tons.

If we take limits of 80 and 120 tons—one standard deviation on either side of the mean—we find that thirty-five out of the fifty-two figures lie between the limits. This is a proportion of 67 per cent; the theory of probability says that for a Normal distribution it should be 68 per cent. This shows quite good agreement but, you may ask, why is it not perfect agreement?

The reason is that our bar chart in Fig. 9 was built up from only fifty-two figures, whereas pure statistical distributions contain an infinitely large number of figures—not just the weekly sales which *did* occur, but all the other possibilities which *might* have occurred within the same general circumstances. The actual sales are a *sample* of these infinite possibilities. For instance, if the sales in Week 43 had been 95 tons instead of 141 tons, the frequency distribution as a whole would hardly be altered at all.

Once we know the mean and standard deviation of a Normal distribution, we can state the probability that any future sales figures will fall within prescribed limits—provided, of course, that the distribution remains unchanged. We can say, for example, that the chance of any single figure being more than 160 tons is so small as to be negligible in practice. To return to our analogy of the archer—his target has a radius of 60 tons and he hardly ever misses it completely.

In working with stocks of unfinished goods which are subject to the uncertain demands of customers, we usually want to know what the maximum sales are likely to be. We already have two possible figures: 141 tons, which was the highest recorded level in 1960, and 160 tons, from the statistical theory of the Normal distribution. Why are these figures different from each other? Because they correspond to different *risk levels*. The chance of sales exceeding 160 tons is only one in seven hundred, whereas the chance of exceeding 141 tons is about one in twenty.

Let us draw the bar chart in Fig. 9 in a different form, so that we can look more closely at these questions of probability and risk levels. First we derive Table VII, which is a cumulative form of Table VI, compiled by adding each figure in the 'Frequency' column to all the preceding ones. This gives the cumulative bar chart in Fig. 10.

It seems as though this chart, like that in Fig. 9, might eventually become a smooth curve if we could obtain enough figures and classify them finely enough. If we try to subdivide Fig. 9 any

TABLE VII: *Weekly sales of chocolic acid in 1970: Cumulative frequency distribution*

Sales not more than (tons)	Frequency	% of Total
29½	0	0
49½	0	0
69½	4	7·7
89½	18	34·6
109½	35	67·3
129½	46	88·5
149½	52	100·0
169½	52	100·0

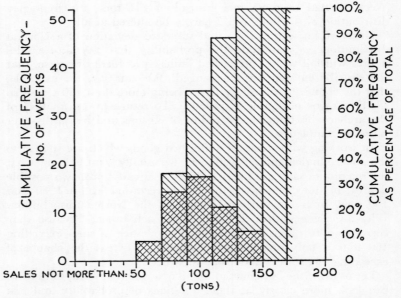

FIG 10 *Weekly Sales of Chocolic Acid. Bar-chart of Cumulative Frequency Distribution*

further, we find that it tends to flatten out into a series of bumps scattered along the horizontal scale, each one unit high: this is not much use to anyone. However, we can make a much smoother curve by subdividing Fig. 10, and we do it in the following way.

TABLE VIII: *Weekly sales of chocolic acid in 1970: Individual sales ranked in ascending order*

Sales not more than (tons)	Rank	Sales not more than (tons)	Rank
55	1	102	27
56	2	103	28
60	3	(103)	29
60	4	103	30
70	5	107	31
76	6	107	32
(80)	7	107	33
80	8	108	34
81	9	109	35
82	10	110	36
84	11	110	37
84	12	112	38
84	13	113	39
86	14	113	40
87	15	114	41
88	16	116	42
89	17	119	43
89	18	122	44
90	19	124	45
90	20	125	46
92	21	131	47
92	22	131	48
95	23	131	49
96	24	132	50
96	25	135	51
101	26	141	52

(Brackets enclose the two figures selected at random and later deleted to round off the total number to fifty.)

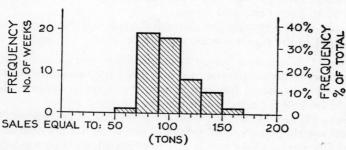

FIG 11 *Skewed Distribution of Sales*

First we arrange all the weekly figures from Table V in ascending order; this is done in Table VIII (page 39). Now we automatically get the cumulative frequencies from the successive numbers in the right-hand column. These are plotted in Fig. 12, and although the horizontal and vertical scales have been turned around, the derivation from Fig. 10 is obvious.

Do not forget that this curve has been derived from sales figures with a Normal distribution and is therefore related to this distribution in some way. It is called 'ogive' of the Normal curve.

The horizontal scale of percentages is divided conventionally into equal divisions. If we were to crowd the centre divisions more closely together and stretch the outside ones apart, we could turn our curved ogive into a straight line. This would be convenient because it is much easier to draw a straight line through a set of points than it is to draw a curved one.

This stretched-out scale is what we find on 'probability' graph paper. For Normal probability paper, the scale is drawn so as to turn the Normal ogive into a straight line. All the statistician's knowledge of the Normal distribution has been put into working out this scale of percentages, and so we can analyse our Normal distribution without having to bother about calculating the standard deviation.

The method of plotting a set of weekly sales figures on probability paper is—

(1) Reject any two figures at random.

(2) Arrange the remaining fifty figures in ascending order of size.

(3) Fit a suitable vertical scale of 'tons per week': a scale ranging from 20 tons to 180 tons will do very well in this case.

(4) Using the bottom scale of percentages, plot the lowest tonnage on the vertical 1 per cent line, the next at 3 per cent, the next at 5 per cent, and so on.

(5) Draw a straight line through the points, giving the greatest weight to the points nearest the middle.

Step (1) is merely a matter of convenience, and is not essential. It is easier to divide 100 per cent into fifty parts than into fifty-two. If we were to use all fifty-two figures, the intervals between them would be 1·92 per cent, which is awkward.

Steps (2) and (4) are based on the reasoning which follows. The lowest weekly figure was 55 tons: this one week is 2 per cent of the total fifty weeks, so we plot it at 1 per cent which is the middle of the 2 per cent slice. It means that 2 per cent of the sales were not

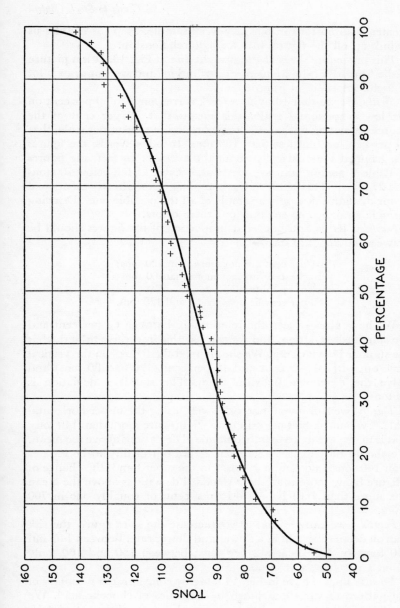

Fig 12 *Sales of Chocolic Acid for 50 weeks of 1970 (Linear Scale)*

greater than 55 tons in our fifty-week sample. Step (5) enables us to link up all the figures into a single relationship.

This procedure gives us the straight line in Fig. 13. It is a picture of the 'spread' of the frequency distribution, and we can draw a lot of useful information from it.

Firstly, we see that 100 tons a week corresponds to 50 per cent on the lower horizontal scale: this means that 50 per cent of the figures are not more than 100 tons; or, reading the upper scale, that 50 per cent are not less than 100 tons. In other words, the figures are grouped symmetrically about the average. In fact, the figures in Table V are not quite symmetrical, because 25 fall below 100 tons and 27 above. This is due to the 'sampling error' already mentioned —our 52 figures are only a sample of all the possible ones. Drawing a single straight line smooths out these errors.

Secondly, let us find out what proportion of the figures should be between 80 and 120 tons—

> 84 per cent are not more than 120 tons;
> 16 per cent are not more than 80 tons;
> so, by subtraction,
> 68 per cent lie between 80 and 120 tons.

We have already seen the relationship between 68 per cent and the standard deviation, and we can use this in reverse to find what the standard deviation is. We simply read the figures on the vertical scale opposite 84 per cent and 16 per cent (120 and 80 tons) and halve the difference between them. The standard deviation is 20 tons.

Thirdly, we can investigate risk levels, using the upper horizontal scale. Two-and-a-half per cent of the figures are more than 140 tons, that is to say, are more than two standard deviations above the mean. We should only expect about one figure out of fifty to be greater than 140 tons, and only one was. On the other hand, the chance of a figure being more than three standard deviations above the mean (i.e. more than 160) is only 0·15 per cent, or roughly one in 700 times.

Fourthly, we can see that as we increase the sales figure, the risk goes on decreasing, but at a slower and slower rate. Between 140 and 150 tons we drop nearly 2 per cent; between 150 and 160, only about $\frac{1}{2}$ per cent, and so on.

To sum up, we have in Fig. 13 a highly concentrated summary of the pattern of variation shown by our sales of chocolic acid. We must not forget, though, that we have only analysed the *unpredictable* variation. In doing so, we have assumed that the average sales will

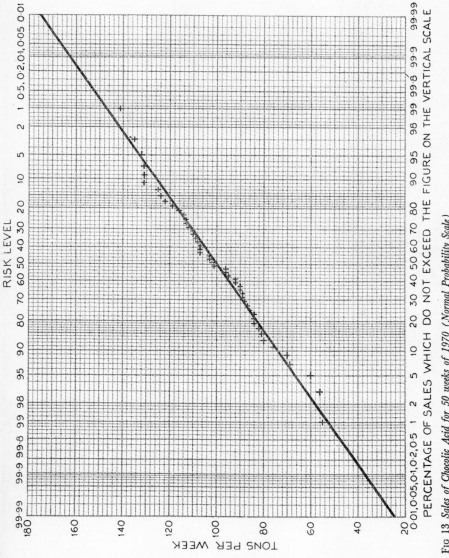

FIG 13 *Sales of Chocolic Acid for 50 weeks of 1970 (Normal Probability Scale)*

not change; later on we shall be looking at situations in which the average does change. Meanwhile, we recall that buffer stocks may be used to absorb this unpredictable variation; we can apply the information in Figure 13 to finding a suitable buffer stock for this particular pattern of sales.

When we analyse the demand in this way, we are studying the variations in quantity—the sales in tons—which occur in a fixed time, one week in our case. Turning to supply, we find the reverse to be true. We shall usually have ordered a fixed quantity, but are uncertain about the exact delivery date. The average interval between placing the order, and receiving the goods is, say, three weeks, but we can expect this to vary a few days either way. If we are exceptionally lucky, we may receive our goods within two weeks of placing the order—or it may be as long as a month in the worst case.

Here is a situation which does not differ fundamentally from the one we have just examined in detail. We can represent the variation in delivery time by a bar chart similar to Fig. 9, but with 'days' or 'weeks' along the horizontal scale. The entire graphical analysis can be continued from this point onwards in exactly the same way as for sales. Strangely enough, this sort of uncertainty has received little attention from the purely theoretical workers in the field of stock control and yet there can be no doubt of its practical importance.

It is buffer stocks which protect us against fluctuations in supply as well as in demand; we shall see in the next chapter how our graphical analysis helps us to calculate them.

Exercises

1. You are told that the weekly sales of diabolone are 20 tons on the average with a standard deviation of 5 tons. How often would you expect the weekly sales to be more than 30 tons?

2. Given a hundred weekly sales figures for diabolone, how many would you expect to lie between 15 tons and 25 tons?

CHAPTER 4

Lead Times and Buffer Stocks

And, had her Stock been less, no doubt
She must have long ago run out.

JONATHAN SWIFT, *Stella's Birthday, 1720.*

Armed with the information from the last chapter, you are asked the following question: "How much stock of chocolic acid must you hold at the beginning of a week to be sure of not running out of stock during that week?"

We already know that you can never be *absolutely* certain of not running out of stock; we also know, from Fig. 13, that with 160 tons to begin with, the chance of not being able to meet sales is so small as to be negligible. Of this 160 tons, you need 100 tons to fill the *expected* sales. The other 60 tons are for protection against maximum sales: they constitute the 'safety stock' or 'buffer stock'. Now it is quite obvious that this size of the buffer stock depends on the risk you are prepared to accept—the risk, that is, of not being able to fill an order.

Supposing an order does arrive when you are out of stock—what action do you take then? There are several possibilities; you may—

(1) Refuse the order; this would lose you the profit on the entire order.

(2) Postpone it; you would then make the profit but lose the goodwill of the customer. The loss of goodwill would almost certainly lead to lost orders and therefore lost profit in the future.

(3) Buy from another dealer and resell; you would retain the goodwill by sacrificing all or part of the immediate profit.

(4) Reduce or rearrange deliveries to other customers; you may be skilful enough to do this so as to lose neither profit nor goodwill, but only at the expense of your own time, which can be valued in terms of money.

There are other ways of dealing with such an emergency, but all have one thing in common: they cost money.

Once again we find ourselves confronted with a problem of balancing one cost against another. On the one hand, we have the cost of holding stock—on the other, the 'cost of running out of stock'. Unfortunately, the cost of running out of stock is not at all easy to work out. It depends on which of the four possible courses of action we decide to take; such a decision is more likely to vary according to the prevailing circumstances than to follow a standard procedure. The cost of the action we decide to take will vary correspondingly, and this would be the estimate of the 'cost of running out of stock'. One company made a gallant attempt to compile such a cost by the following procedure—

(1) List all the alternative actions which might ensue from a stock-out.
(2) Estimate the cost of each.
(3) Estimate the probability of each.
(4) Multiply (2) by (3) for each alternative.
(5) Add the separate products from (4): the sum is the cost of running out.

Considerable difficulties attend steps (2) and (3). In the former, costing the long-term effects of emergency action may be almost impossible: 'loss of goodwill' may be only one of many such effects. There is an added complication in that the *duration* of the stock-out may have to come under scrutiny: a delay of two weeks will probably annoy a customer more than twice as much as a one-week delay.

There are two approaches to (3). Traditional statistics such as we have used up to now, equates 'probability' with 'relative frequency', so if past records of emergency action are available and it is reasonable to expect the same pattern of behaviour in the future, the probabilities can be measured. In my experience, this quantitative ideal has never been attained, nor do I know of any recorded case. Imagine a Sales Manager saying, "Half the time we get Blodger's to help out (and we do the same for them when we have to); about a third of the stock-outs are covered by splitting consignments; the rest usually depend on me smoothing the customer down." Then, if you succeed, imagine costing these three!

If probabilities *are* used, they are generally subjective ones, and the study of them has opened up a whole new area of statistical methods called 'statistical inference'. Theory abounds and different schools of thought maintain a vigorous debate; unfortunately it is not matched by practical trials in the realms of stock control. Thus we come to the alternative approach—the guess.

"An educated guess," said General Patton, "is just as accurate and quicker than compiled error"; and a guess may well be needed at this point—but it must be an *educated* one. Since we are to guess,

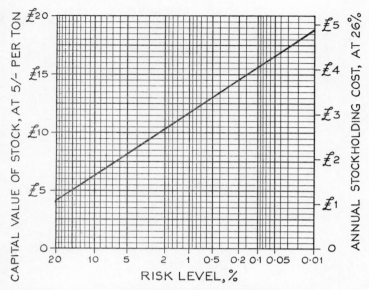

Fɪɢ 14 *Cost of Buffer Stock for One Week's Protection, at Various Risk Levels*

we may as well guess the risk level directly rather than compile it from an equally subjective "cost of running out of stock".

Fig. 14 will help. It reproduces part of Fig. 13, but with the vertical scale showing the stockholding cost instead of the sales tonnage. The vertical scale is the 'insurance premium', and the horizontal one the risk. Now you can use your judgment in an educated way and decide where to fix the risk level. Suppose you decide that 2 per cent is a reasonable risk to take, implying that you would be out of stock during one week of the year, then your decision sets the buffer stock at 41 tons.

You may decide at the same time that this 2 per cent shall apply to all stocks of a similar type. Then the drudgery of working out the buffer stocks can be delegated and the figure of 2 per cent becomes an important statement of general policy. It resembles the rate of return which was the policy decision for economic batch sizes. Fig. 13 and 14 show how changes in policy about risk-taking will affect stock levels and stockholding costs.

Returning to details again, let us suppose that we want to provide enough stock to cover us for two weeks instead of one, using the same risk level of 2 per cent. First we must obviously have the 200

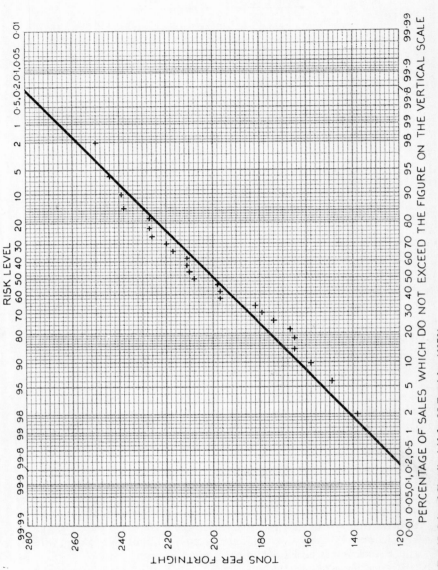

Fig 15 *Sales of Chocolic Acid for 25 Fortnights (1970)*

tons needed to meet the expected sales, but what about the buffer stock? If it was 41 tons for one week, will it be 82 tons for two weeks? Common sense tells us that it will not, because maximum sales are not likely to occur in each of two successive weeks.

We could, of course, plot the fortnightly sales instead of the weekly figures on probability paper; this has been done in Fig. 15, from which we can read off the buffer stock as 58 tons. "Surely," you may say, "this is a tedious business. We have gone to a lot of trouble to derive Fig. 13. Do we have to do it all over again just to change the number of weeks?"

Fortunately, we do not. There is a simple rule for finding the buffer stock for any number of weeks. Simply multiply the buffer stock for one week by the square root of the number of weeks. For our chocolic acid example, we have—

> Buffer stock for one week = 41 tons
> For two weeks, square root = 1·414
> Buffer stock for two weeks = (41 × 1·414) tons
> = 58 tons

which confirms the estimate we got from Fig. 15.

One most important point must be made about this question of buffer stocks. If we begin a two-week period with a stock of 258 tons, then the chance of running out of stock *in the first week* is infinitesimally small; our effective buffer stock is 158 tons! Our calculated risk of 2 per cent applies to the two-week period *as a whole* and is not spread evenly throughout the period.

I have explained this method of calculating buffer stocks in full. This was necessary in order to introduce the statistical principles behind it, since it is principles which are emphasized in this book. Nevertheless, it is an equally sound principle that the methods described shall be workable in practice.

If you are running a factory which makes only a few main products, a detailed analysis of each is feasible; it is also desirable that we look more closely at the period over which the stocks are to provide cover against uncertainty; it is known as the *lead time*.

The Lead Time

The Lead Time in terms of stock control, is the interval between making a decision about stock and achieving the consequent result in the stock itself. In general, the decision will be to order some replenishment and the achievement will be, not merely its arrival but its *availability* for the next process.

The Lead Time is insufficiently discussed in most of the technical

3

books. The authors of such books generally seem to assume that
either the reader already knows what the term means or that it is
identifiable with the delivery time. The supplier's delivery time is,
however, only one component of the total lead time, the others
including such matters as the preparation of an order and the
process of receiving the material when it is delivered. The latter in
turn may include such items as unloading, checking or counting,
inspecting or testing, and carrying out clerical operations.

To define the lead time correctly and investigate it critically can
be a most important preliminary to the more orthodox statistical
methods of stock control. Indeed, I know of a case in which the
saving in stock effected by diminishing the lead time proved to be
equal to that subsequently achieved by more elaborate statistical
methods. In this case, the lead time had three main components;
they were—

Shipment (delivery time)	4 weeks
Correspondence	1 week
Forecasting requirements	3 weeks
TOTAL	8 weeks

Thus the total lead time was 8 weeks, just twice the actual
delivery time. The latter was the time taken by the cargo vessel to
go half-way around the world; at one time during the investigation
air freight was considered but was rejected for good reasons. The
first point the investigator picked upon was the correspondence.
This was by letter post and took about a week. He suggested that
a cable taking only a few hours and costing about £1, would be a
trivial addition to the expenditure and would, through the
consequent reduction in lead time, more than pay for itself by
reducing the stock level.

At this point, though, a complication crept in. The replenishment
of stock was by a constant-cycle system (*see* page 85), the cycle
being monthly. It turned out that the determination of requirements was carried out by several senior executives of the organization and Parkinson's Law applied. In other words, the work to be
done expanded to fill the time available and there was no sense of
urgency beyond this. To cut a long story short, it turned out that
there would be no effective saving unless a *complete* month was
saved. Nevertheless, the simultaneous introduction of both cables
and 'automatic forecasting' did manage to save one month.

The automatic forecasting was of the simplest type: it consisted
of the method of exponential smoothing described in Chapter 7.

The latter took only a few minutes work instead of three weeks and demanded a much lower level of skill. Moreover, it actually gave slightly better results![1] Not only in forecasting, but in all documentary procedures associated with additions to and withdrawals from stock, unnecessary delays can inflate stock levels as well as being undesirable in themselves. However, the time a supplier takes to deliver a replenishment will usually be the major component of the lead time and deserves some attention here.

Delivery Time
All too often, a customer accepts without question the manufacturer's quoted delivery time. Much can often be achieved by bargaining or discussion. I remember one exasperated manager telling me that his reason for high stocks was slow delivery, caused by the company for which he worked having got on the wrong side of a senior employee—a lady, as it happened—of the suppliers. His remedy for reducing stocks was that the Company should allow him to entertain the lady at its expense, the which being done, he undertook to persuade her to give a better service. His estimate of the reduction in delivery time which could be brought about by the consequent goodwill was from 30 days to 10 days. It may seem odd that such psychological factors should creep into stock control, which so many people identify with 'soulless technique', but there are many managerial matters in which goodwill and co-operation can often impart benefits to both sides.

Handling and Inspection
Once delivery time and documentation have been dealt with, there remain the activities associated with handling and those brought about by the need to inspect consignments. The former may be improved by Work Study, supplemented by a knowledge of mechanical handling; the one without the other may only lead to more efficient ways of doing unnecessary work.

Unloading and handling may include elementary checks like weighing or counting the consignment which are also capable of being improved by simple work study, but when chemical or physical characteristics need testing, further benefits may be gained from statistical quality control. It is no longer taken for granted that every consignment should undergo 100 per cent inspection, so a calculated sampling plan can reduce the lead time. Once again we

[1] A comparison of the two methods is given in *Sales Forecasting* by A. Battersby (Cassell, 1968), page 14.

have a matter in which "a little learning is a dangerous thing" and expert guidance is recommended. Also, modern managers no longer accept the absolute necessity for inspecting a consignment twice— on despatch and on receipt. The more refined methods of statistical control developed in the U.S.A. by Dodge and Romig enable mutually-agreed specifications to be drawn up together with a referee system that makes a *single* inspection adequate in that it satisfies both parties. This is one example of the benefits of inter-company co-operation. There are others, as the following example will show.

Inter-Company Co-operation

I was once asked to help a Company with its storage problems, with particular reference to the storage of its finished stocks. It appeared that more storage capacity was needed, and this might be available in the form of tanks used for the storage of raw materials. The Company was engaged on the cyclic manufacture of three products A, B and C and depended for the manufacture of these materials on three raw materials which we will call for convenience *a*, *b* and *c*. Each of these raw materials had a delivery time of two weeks, effectively equal to the total lead time because the supplier was very close to the customer and the other items of lead time were, in this case, negligible. A discussion with the supplier elicited the fact that his delivery time was based on his own manufacturing cycle in which *a*, *b* and *c* were made successively in a cycle of one fortnight. At certain times in his cycle, therefore, he was able to give *immediate* delivery of one of these raw materials—the one which happened to be under manufacture at the moment.

The customer himself was using a manufacturing cycle of three weeks, a supposedly optimum cycle which balanced the cost of changing over from one product to another against the cost of holding stocks (see Appendix 4). In the broader sense, however, it was not the best cycle. The upshot of the investigation was that the two companies synchronized their manufacturing cycles and because of this, the customer's bulk storage of raw material was no longer necessary. Thus raw material storage tanks were made available for finished products. (This account does not disclose *why* the extra storage for finished products was necessary in the first place but that, as Kipling would have said, is another story.)

Variable Lead Times

The lead time usually varies slightly but can often be taken as fixed for all practical purposes. When this is not so, it may be dealt with by statistical methods as described later in this chapter. A recent development in stock control theory has been that which allows a randomly varying lead time to be considered in conjunction with a randomly varying offtake. This is discussed at some length in Chapter 9.

Method Study of Lead Time

A Method Study analysis of the lead time, similar to that discussed in Appendix 1, can lead to its reduction with a consequent saving in buffer stock. Although this cannot always be done for every single item, it is obviously worth while for the major ones because the payoff for each individual material supplied is high enough to justify the expense of the analysis. When the number of products is high, the 'Pareto' (or 'ABC') method described in Chapter 7 may be helpful, or it might be possible to analyse *groups* rather than individuals. Thus, one paint factory analyses its sales only for each colour of paint as an aggregate; the various sizes of tin are dealt with in cruder ways. There is nothing to be ashamed of in using short-cut methods, although at the risk of repetition, I would emphasize the wisdom of consulting an expert statistician who also knows (or can find out) the local circumstances within which any such rules are drawn up, the conditions in which they will be used and the people who will apply them.

Quick Methods for finding Buffer Stocks

(1) If the parameter being studied, say the sales or the lead time, is known or assumed to follow the Poisson distribution law, detailed analysis is unnecessary because the standard deviation may be deduced from the average (the arithmetical mean). It is, in fact, equal to the square root of the mean. The Poisson distribution, unlike the Normal, is not symmetrical but gives a lopsided or skewed bar-chart. It tends to give a good fit to the data when the unit accounting period for sales is very short—a day, say, rather than a week—or when the demand tends to be for one article at a time. The classic example of the latter case is newspapers when sold retail, so it occurs in many early articles on stock control as "The Newsboy Problem". It is also appropriate to spare parts and, we may reasonably suppose, to items of high unit cost like electronic computers.

Lead times themselves may follow a variety of distributions, and because negative lead times are impossible, the Normal distribution is unlikely. Nevertheless, it may be used for convenience, as may also the Poisson. Table IX is an example of a distributed lead time: it describes a situation in which supplies of chocolic acid are received about four weeks (each of 6 working days) after the order is placed. An analysis of the last fifty orders gave the frequencies as tabulated.

TABLE IX: *Lead times for chocolic acid: frequency distribution*

Period (days)	Frequency
20	0
21	3
22	7
23	9
24	11
25	12
26	5
27	2
28	1
	Total 50

TABLE X: *Sales of chocolic acid over several weeks*

No. of Weeks	SALES IN TONS		
	Expected	Minimum	Maximum
1	100	59	141
2	200	142	258
3	300	229	371
4	400	318	482
5	500	408	592

Their average is 24 days: in round figures, its square root is 5 and so if the distribution is Poisson its standard deviation would be about 5 days. A rough-and-ready rule might consist of simply multiplying this by a universal risk factor—a policy factor—of 2, giving a buffer stock of 10 days to cover the uncertainties of the lead time. As it happens, the Poisson distribution does not fit the data in Table IX very well: the figures are more or less symmetrically disposed about their mean and have a calculated standard deviation equal to 1·6 days. It follows that the Poisson distribution in this case gives a rather generous buffer stock.

Using more sophisticated methods, one group of operational

researchers tackled a variable-lead-time problem in such a way as to release £100,000 of working capital.[1]

(2) We can also use the difference between the highest and lowest weekly (or monthly) sales as a short cut to finding buffer stocks. Although we rejected the range as inefficient, its use can be justified when we are prepared to forfeit some accuracy for the sake of speed.

We begin with the typical set of sales figures given in Table V. The range for the last thirteen weeks of 1970 was from 56 to 151 tons, that is, 85 tons. Standard statistical tables tell us that multiplying this by 0·3 will give us an estimate of the standard deviation. In this case the estimate is $25\frac{1}{2}$ tons. We can see that this is very rough by comparing it with the true standard deviation, 20 tons. We could have made a better estimate by taking the *average* range for the four quarters of 1970: this is $68\frac{1}{2}$ tons and would give a standard deviation of $20\frac{1}{2}$ tons. You may ask why we do not use the range over the entire year. The reason is that this method becomes very unreliable if we take the range over more than about a dozen figures.

You will remember that we found the 2 per cent buffer stock to be 41 tons. This 41 tons is the standard deviation multiplied by a factor of 2·05, and we could have found this factor also from standard statistical tables had we not used the simpler graphical method. We can combine the two figures 0·3 and 2·05 into a single factor 0·615 by multiplying them together. Since we are using an approximate method, we may as well round this off to 0·6.

The rule for finding the buffer stock is then—

(1) Find the range of sales over the last 13 weeks.
(2) Multiply by 0·6.
(3) Multiply the result by the square root of the number of weeks for which protection is required.

This is another case in which it is advisable to consult a statistician when devising the system.

Positive and Negative Buffer Stocks

The buffer stock we have looked at up to now has been a *positive* one, its purpose being to cover a possible *excess* of sales over some expected estimate. However, as Figs. 13 and 15 reveal, sales may also fall short and thereby create a risk of inadequate room for the replenishment when it arrives. The embarrassment caused by such

---

[1] Colcutt, R.H., Banbury, Massey and Ward, "A Method of Fixing Desirable Stock Levels and of Stock Control", *Operational Research Quarterly*, June 1959, page 81.

a lack may extend to a monetary cost. For example, demurrage may have to be paid if railway wagons or other means of transport are delayed, or some emergency warehouse space may have to be rented. There is therefore a close resemblance to a 'stock-out' and the unfortunate merchant in such a predicament may be said to have too small a 'stock' of space.

The possible need for space may be calculated by the method just described and is therefore called a *negative buffer stock*. Table X provides a basis for calculating a negative stock of this sort, in that it gives *minimum* sales as well as maxima; it was compiled on the assumption of a symmetrical (Gaussian) distribution and a 2 per cent risk level for the minimum as well as the maximum sales. It follows that the minimum is always as much below the expected value as the maximum is above it, but this need not always be so. The cost of inadequate space will almost certainly be different from the cost of inadequate stock—for one thing, it is more likely to be known exactly—so the negative and positive risk levels may be set differently.

Exercises

1. "If delivery takes 8 weeks, we must order 8 weeks' stock at a time." Show why this commonly-held belief is not true.

2. If the lead time for chocolic acid were to increase to 3 weeks and there were no other changes, what buffer stock would be required?

3. With a lead time of 2 weeks, what should be the negative buffer stock for diabolone? (See Chapter 3, Exercise 1: the distribution is known to be Normal.)

CHAPTER 5

Sales Forecasting

> Figuring the nature of the times deceas'd
> The which observ'd, a man may prophesy,
> With a near aim, of the main chance of things
> As yet not come to life . . .
>
> SHAKESPEARE, *King Henry IV* (Part II).

Forecasting is used in practically every facet of a company's business, although many forecasts are not recognized as such. For example, an engineer who says that a boiler will not burst in service is making a forecast of its performance. Why do we not include this type of statement in the common idea of a forecast? I suggest that it is because it expresses what is, to all intents and purposes, a practical certainty. The sort of thing which we think of in connexion with the word 'forecast' is something which contains a fairly large element of uncertainty or error. This suggestion is the basis for the first main point of this chapter, which is that a forecast is a statement about the future *which is wrong*.

The second important point is that no forecast is of any interest in itself, except as an intellectual exercise. In industrial transactions, the *action* which is taken as a result of a forecast is the important thing. By acknowledging the existence of errors and making the action suitable to them as well as to the forecast itself, we begin the evolution of a control system; this is dealt with as the third main point in this chapter.

If we leave aside religious and supernatural experiences, we can say that no one can foretell the future with absolute accuracy. A forecast is a projection into the future of experience from the past; this experience may be either factual (a record of past sales) or intuitive (the sales manager's knowledge of his customers). The best forecast will be made when the greatest possible amount of information of both types is used. It rarely is in practice because the forecast has to be produced in a reasonably short time with a limited staff. This means that we must ignore some of the information and the error is thereby made greater.

Because a forecast has proved to be incorrect, there is a tendency for its originator to feel ashamed of the error and for the recipient to be scornful of its inaccuracy. In fact, the fault lies not with the forecaster but rather with the system, which is only equipped to deal with an absolutely correct forecast: this cannot be achieved except by a rare fluke. Methods which do allow for errors are in existence, as we have already seen in the preceding chapters, but their operation is very imperfectly understood and has only recently been the subject of close study.

The methods used for forecasting may be classified under two main headings—synthetic and analytical. The sales manager who makes his forecast by considering what each of the individual customers is likely to buy and adding up the answers is making the *synthetic* type of forecast. If, however, he draws a graph of total sales

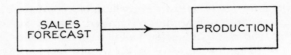

FIG 16

in the recent past and extends this graph into the future, this is *analytical* forecasting. In practice, one finds that the best forecasts are made by combining the two methods. The sales manager may say, "Generally speaking, I expect sales to go on much as before [analytical], except that Fiddle & Fake are going out of business [synthetic]. On the other hand, the market as a whole has generally shown a seasonal increase at this time of year [analytical] and Fooles Ltd. tell me that they expect to be doubling their requirements [synthetic]."

One advantage of the analytical method is that it enables the errors to be estimated. This is not so with the synthetic method, because even if we put upper and lower limits to each customer's requirements, we cannot add up these upper and lower limits since they may not all be fulfilled at the same time.

This estimate of the error should really be considered as a part of the forecast itself and, as mentioned above, the action to be taken should depend upon *both* figures.

The second point mentioned earlier is that the forecast is only important when taken in association with the action which it causes. In other words, the forecast is part of a control system, which in its simplest form may be as shown in Fig. 16. (The arrow in Fig. 16, as in all subsequent diagrams of this type, means 'affects' and also means that there is some delay: the word 'forecast' is implied by the arrow and will be dropped.) Very simple systems of this sort are rare, but an example is provided by the generation and distribution of electricity. The electricity authority calculates a demand curve from past experience and sees that generators are ready to be brought in to meet peak loads. They are forced to do this because there is no way of holding A.C. electricity in stock.

The system may be extended to include buying as shown in Fig. 17.

Fig 17

The buying orders are placed on the basis of the production forecast, which in turn is based on the sales forecast. Each forecast is limited by the one which follows it—the sales forecast must be within the limits of productive capacity, and we can only produce if there is enough raw material. Buying can therefore affect sales and this state of affairs is shown in Fig. 18.

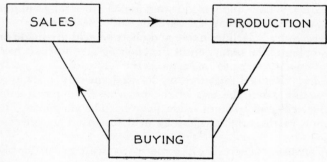

Fig 18

Someone has to start the chain—usually the sales department. Information will flow around the circle and eventually settle down to a level which is equal to the lowest restriction. A typical process would be—

Sales: "We could sell 6,500 tons of chocolic acid this year."

Production: "The plant is capable of making 8,000 tons a year: we approve the sales forecast."

Buying: "We can only buy enough raw material to make 5,200 tons of chocolic acid."

Sales: "The sales forecast is amended to 5,200 tons."

From this point onwards the forecast will remain steady at 5,200 tons until more information is available.

In practice, our control systems are much more complicated than this. Fig. 19 shows how one part of a control system may be linked to another.

Sales: "We can sell 1,500 tons of garlium oxide a year."

[Garlium oxide is another imaginary compound. Any chemist would know that it combines with chocolic acid to produce garlic chocolate!]

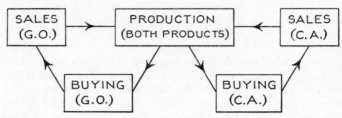

FIG 19

Production: "We only have capacity for 400 tons."

Buying: "The supply of raw material is practically unlimited."

Sales: "Sales forecast for garlium oxide: 400 tons."

Production: "Garlium oxide and chocolic acid are made on the same plant. The reduction in the chocolic acid forecast has now freed enough plant to make the extra 1,100 tons."

Sales: "Revised sales forecast for garlium oxide: 1,500 tons."

Even this is not the end of the process—the forecast sales for chocolic acid and garlium oxide have become stabilized, but the reduction in the original chocolic acid forecast may affect other circuits—

Production: "There is still some spare capacity on the plant—we could make more jekaldehyde if sales and buying agree," and so on.

These interlinked circuits form a complicated network of communications within the company. A new or revised forecast is a 'disturbance' or 'signal' which can cause other disturbances throughout the entire system. The process is rather like throwing a stone into a pond—the effect is not confined to the point where the stone enters the water, but spreads throughout the pond as ripples. The ripples gradually die away as they get farther from the source of the disturbance. Similarly, a change in the forecast for a process has its greatest effect on the adjacent stocks and processes and spreads outwards with diminishing effect.

We are left with a compromise between the tidy isolated system shown in Fig. 18 and the sprawling mass of interlinked circuits just mentioned. The former is too simple to bear much resemblance to the real situation and the latter is too complicated to handle. Such organizational problems are combined with investigations of the nervous systems of animals and the design of servo-mechanisms in the studies called 'cybernetics'.

Next we deal with the third main point referred to above, beginning with a discussion of a control system, then going on to show how

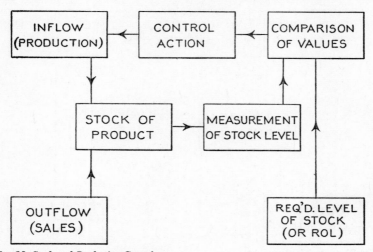

FIG 20 *Stock and Production Control*

forecasting (both of averages and errors) affects the system when it is introduced.

The error-controlled system shown in Figs. 20 and 21 occurs frequently both in its natural and artificial forms. These two figures show how the general shape of the system remains the same in two very different applications. (They are, I hope, self-explanatory: remember that an arrow means 'affects' and does not indicate a direction of flow.)

First look at Fig. 21: this is a control system for the central heating of a house. As heat is lost through the walls, the temperature falls. The temperature is measured and a part of the control system compares it with the setting on the thermostat, say 65 degrees Fahrenheit. If the temperature is above 65 degrees, the boiler is turned down, and vice versa.

One of the difficulties about designing this type of system is the *delay*. Heating up a building is a slow process, and even after the boiler has started the house will go on getting cooler before the full effect of the boiler has been felt. The temperature will tend to rise and fall regularly instead of remaining steady. In a badly-designed system, this fluctuation may get quite out of hand, so that the house becomes alternately an igloo and a Turkish bath, while the controller desperately tries to catch up with itself.

A stock of product can, and often does, behave in the same way.

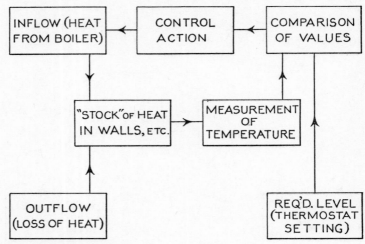

Fɪɢ 21 *Central Heating Control*

Stock is built up to a high level so that production has to be stopped; a heavy sales demand may then use up most of the stock before production can be built up again. By the time maximum production is available the sales may have settled down to their normal level and the excess stock begins to build up again. We shall have an unstable system such as is described in Chapter 6.

Instrument engineers have many ingenious ways of dealing with these symptoms of delay. For central heating, one solution is to put a controller *outside* the house. As frost begins to form outside, the external controller turns up the boiler. The frost causes heat to leak away from the walls more quickly, but the boiler is already giving out more heat. The outside controller has *forecast* a fall in the inside temperature or 'stock of heat' and has thereby averted it. In doing so, it has *stabilized* the inside temperature, just as a good sales forecast will help to stabilize the stock and help production to run smoothly. Such a forecast is indicated in Fig. 22 by the heavy vertical arrow which shows forecast sales affecting production.

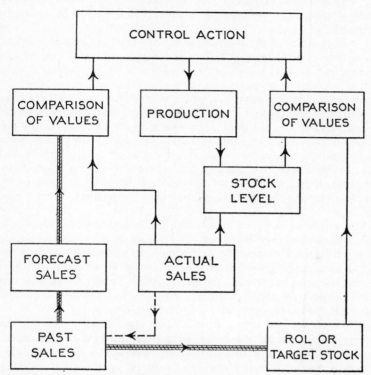

Fig 22 *Stock and Production Control System with Forecasting*

The analogy with the central heating system has been pursued at some length, because it is a very close one. In fact, there are many points of resemblance between the analogue computers which can be used to study the behaviour of stock systems and the control instruments of the central heating type.

Suppose that a careless engineer has connected the outside thermometer the wrong way round. The behaviour of the temperature will depend on the relative strengths of the signals from the inside and outside controllers. The boiler may continue to work in a satisfactory manner, but it may also go out and stay out, or stay on indefinitely, or start to produce the widely fluctuating temperatures

which we are trying to avoid. This reversal of connexions is equivalent to predicting a fall in sales and then finding that they rise. If this
happens the stock system may also become unstable. By extending
our simple control system to include a forecasting control, we have
made it even more necessary to ensure that it should be properly
designed.

We have reached the point at which the analogy begins to break
down. The central heating system is complete in itself, but, as was
pointed out earlier, a production and stock control system is only
part of a complex organization. Any instability will set up disturbances in neighbouring systems, which will usually tend to react so as
to restore order. Besides, the system itself contains sensible human
beings, who can adjust themselves and who are not likely to let the
situation get completely out of hand. One can hardly imagine a
human production controller calling for chocolic acid when he was
already overstocked with it: if he did, an outside influence (the factory
manager, most probably) would begin to stabilize the system by
gently correcting the production controller or sending him on a long
holiday.

The effect of this sort of control by interconnected systems is
called 'multi-stability' by cyberneticians, for obvious reasons—even
so, it is still better to have the individual systems as stable as possible.
In plain language, if the production controller says "Ah, well, it will
all sort itself out in the end," he will probably be right—but one can
hardly expect the factory manager to enjoy the sorting-out process
if it calls for his personal and frequent intervention.

Although we are trying to minimize the need for this human
intervention, we shall never succeed in doing away entirely with the
need for it. The information which leads to synthetic sales forecasting
generally reaches the sales manager in a haphazard fashion—a paragraph in *The Financial Times*, an indiscreet remark at lunch, or a
casual inquiry by telephone. No automatic forecasting system can
hope to duplicate the experienced man's unique ability to marshal
these disorganized facts and make sensible deductions from them.
Should we conclude, then, that automatic systems are a waste of
effort?

I think not, for two reasons. *First*, because statistical analysis can
summarize the past figures into a convenient and helpful form—
this in itself is valuable information, and we are not justified in
rejecting *anything* which can help to make our forecasts more reliable.
Second, because the sales manager will be faced with a long list of
forecasts to be prepared each month, and perhaps three-quarters of
these will only require straightforward projections from the preceding

period. In producing an automatic forecast of these, we can free the sales manager from a mass of humdrum routine and leave him free to devote extra effort to the forecasts which really need his individual attention.

The man who budgets his household expenses on an intelligent forecast, and who keeps a careful comparison of his expected and actual expenditures, can keep a much lower average balance in his current account than the man who has no proper records and pays each bill as it turns up. The current account represents our working stock of money, and working stocks of materials can be reduced by exactly the same tactics. The capital released can be transferred to our 'deposit account' of productive investment, giving greater earning power. All this, then, is based on one first step—the frank admission that no forecaster is infallible, coupled with the recognition of stocks as part of a definite mechanism which calls for control.

I have tried to emphasize the need to consider the *purpose* of a forecast before setting out to prepare it. Let us now look briefly at the methods used for forecasting. For our purposes in the field of stock control, we can confine ourselves to *short-term* forecasts for controlling the day-to-day operations of a business; the long-term projections of the economist, which take in such factors as population growth and economic development, are of much less interest to us. A short-term forecast is, by its very nature, one which must be revised frequently; furthermore, we probably have to make forecasts for each of a wide range of goods. It is therefore important that the method we choose be *quick*. In general, this means that the method must be *simple*. (This is not true when an efficient computer is available, but this development will come under consideration when Chapter 10 is reached.)

We shall be applying one common method of projecting or 'extrapolating' the past into the future—that is, the moving average in Chapter 6. We shall use a moving average taken over thirteen weeks to generate sales forecasts for Figs. 33 and 34. Let us examine the method here by considering the same set of weekly sales figures as will be used in these diagrams. They are given in Table XI, which is a continuation of Table V on page 34. These sales figures were generated artificially, those for the first and last quarters being drawn from a frequency distribution with a mean value of 100 tons —the same distribution as for Table V. The sales for the second and third quarters were compiled from similar Normal distributions but with means of 80 and 120 tons respectively.

In some ways it is a pity that we are using artificial values, because a set of sales figures from a real-life situation would have been more

TABLE XI: *Weekly sales of chocolic acid in tons 1971*

First Quarter			Second Quarter			Third Quarter			Fourth Quarter		
Mth.	Wk.	Sales	Mth.	Wk.	Sales	Mth.	Wk.	Sales	Mth.	Wk.	Sales
	1	76		14	63		27	97		40	131
Jan.	2	78	Apr.	15	68	Jul.	28	120	Oct.	41	79
	3	110		16	73		29	138		42	99
	4	87		17	86		30	116		43	116
	5	100		18	69		31	147		44	95
Feb.	6	102	May	19	79	Aug.	32	89	Nov.	45	67
	7	81		20	49		33	115		46	121
	8	108		21	79		34	128		47	112
	9	84		22	82		35	115		48	89
	10	127		23	73		36	132		49	95
Mar.	11	114	Jun.	24	86	Sep.	37	76	Dec.	50	96
	12	98		25	82		38	114		51	129
	13	115		26	86		39	92		52	69
Total		1,280	Total		975	Total		1479	Total		1,298
Average		98	Average		75	Average		114	Average		100
(Range		51)	(Range		37)	(Range		71)	(Range		64)

Grand Total 5,032
Average for the Year 97
(Overall Range 98)

convincing. The advantage of these synthetic figures is that we *know* that their average falls sharply at the end of the first quarter, jumps 40 tons at the end of the second quarter, and so on. We also know that the other variations are random ones: we know these things are so because we deliberately made them so. This arrangement gives us a good basis for studying the effectiveness of the various methods of forecasting.

In these examples we are taking a moving average over 13 weeks. Naturally enough, this takes 13 weeks to respond completely to each stepwise change in sales. If we had taken our moving average over only 4 weeks, then it would have completely adjusted itself to the new value in 4 weeks; on the other hand, a 52-week average would never entirely adjust itself to the quarterly changes in Table XI, because they do not persist for long enough to allow it to do so. Moving averages for 4, 13 and 52 weeks are shown in Figure 23, in comparison with the weekly figures of Table XI.

The shorter the period, the more rapid the response—but, as always, this advantage is accompanied by a drawback. The shorter the period, the less is the extent to which random variations are smoothed out. We can see this in Fig. 23, and also by considering a moving 'average' of one week only, in which case the whole of the random variation would be passed on in the forecast. The best period for any particular set of figures is usually found by trial and error after taking into account such factors as seasonal and other trends.

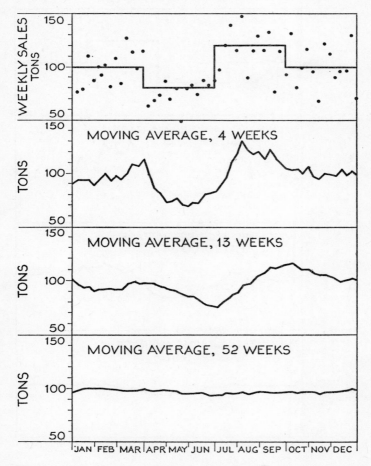

Fig 23 *Unweighted Moving Averages—Effect of Smoothing Period on Random Variations and Response to Changes in Level of Sales*

We do not calculate afresh each week by adding up all the 13 figures, but rather by adjusting the value for the previous week. For example, the first quarter in Table XI gives a total of 1,280 tons, from which we derive an average of 98 tons: this is our forecast of future sales after Week 13. To obtain the new total for Week 14, we add in the sales figure for that week, 63 tons, and subtract the sales for Week 1, 76 tons. The new total is 1,267 tons, giving a new

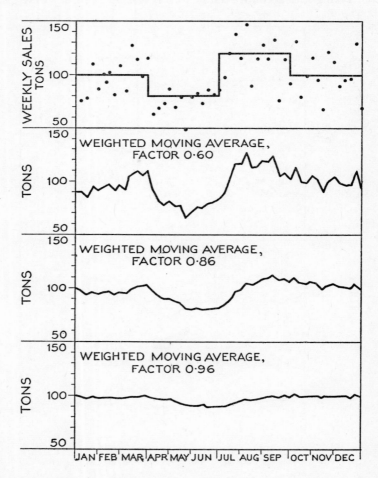

FIG 24 *Weighted Moving Averages—Effect of Weighting Factor on Random Variations and Response to Changes in Level of Sales*

average of 97 tons when divided by 13. In order to adjust our forecasts in this way, we need to keep a record of all the 13 figures which
make up the current total: forecasting would be much simpler if we
could find a way of working from the total alone.

A second objection to moving totals might be expressed like this:
"Last week's sales figure is much more recent than one which was
taken three months ago. Ought we not to recognize this in some
way, by making the recent figure more important than the older
ones?"

There is a simple forecasting rule which answers both these objec-
tions. It is this: "Take two factors which add up to one. Multiply the
forecast of this week's sales by the first factor and the actual sales this
week by the second factor. Add the two results to obtain the new
forecast." Although two factors are mentioned, choosing either one
will automatically set the other, because they must add up to one.
When we refer to 'the factor', we shall mean the one which multi-
plies the previous forecast.

Let us see how this works in practice, using a factor of 0·6. Suppose we enter 1971 with a forecast of 100 tons a week. The first
week's sales are 76 tons and the new forecast is calculated from—

$$
\begin{array}{rcl}
 & & \text{tons} \\
0\cdot4 \times 76 \text{ tons} & = & 30\cdot4 \\
0\cdot6 \times 100 \text{ tons} & = & 60\cdot0 \\
\hline
\text{New forecast} & = & 90\cdot4 \\
\end{array}
$$

The actual sales in the second week are 78 tons and the new forecast is—

$$
\begin{array}{rcl}
 & & \text{tons} \\
0\cdot4 \times 78 \text{ tons} & = & 31\cdot2 \\
0\cdot6 \times 90\cdot4 \text{ tons} & = & 54\cdot2 \\
\hline
\text{New forecast} & = & 85\cdot4 \\
\end{array}
$$

which we can also write as—

$$
\begin{array}{rcl}
 & & \text{tons} \\
0\cdot4 \times 1 \times 78 & = & 31\cdot2 \\
0\cdot4 \times 0\cdot6 \times 76 & = & 18\cdot2 \\
0\cdot6 \times 0\cdot6 \times 100 & = & 36\cdot0 \\
\hline
\text{New forecast} & = & 85\cdot4 \\
\end{array}
$$

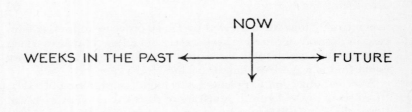

WEEKS IN THE PAST ← NOW → FUTURE

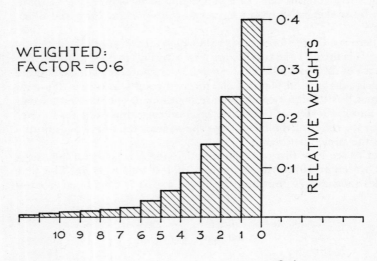

WEIGHTED:
FACTOR = 0·6

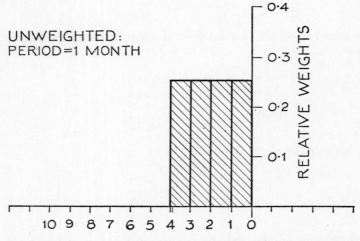

UNWEIGHTED:
PERIOD = 1 MONTH

FIG 25 *Relative Weights for Weekly Sales in the Past—for Weighted and Unweighted Averages*

As we continue in this way the importance or 'weight' of the original forecast of 100 tons gradually dies away. At the end of nine weeks, the new forecast is made up from the elements shown below—

					tons
0·4	× 1·000	×	84	=	33·6
0·4	× 0·600	×	108	=	25·9
0·4	× 0·360	×	81	=	11·7
0·4	× 0·216	×	102	=	8·8
0·4	× 0·130	×	100	=	5·2
0·4	× 0·078	×	87	=	2·7
0·4	× 0·047	×	110	=	2·1
0·4	× 0·028	×	78	=	0·9
0·4	× 0·017	×	76	=	0·5
	0·010	×	100	=	1·0

New forecast = 92·4

It is easy to see how the relative importance of each week becomes less as one goes farther into the past. Their relative weights are shown diagrammatically in Fig. 25 (page 70), and you can see that they build up a smooth curve which gradually dies away. This is called an 'exponential' curve, and this type of forecasting is called the method of exponentially weighted moving averages—a rather cumbersome title for what is essentially a simple method.

When using an *unweighted* moving average, we achieved a balance between its speed of response and smoothing effect by choosing the number of weeks: for exponentially weighted averages we choose the factor instead; a high weighting factor will correspond to a large number of weeks. Fig. 24 (page 68) shows moving averages calculated from Table XI with weighting factors of 0·60, 0·86 and 0·96. These factors were chosen because they correspond roughly in their smoothing effect to the 4, 13 and 52 weeks of Fig. 23.

Exponentially weighted moving averages are coming into use on an increasing scale for short-term forecasting. The method is quick and convenient, demanding only three figures at any time (present week's sales, previous forecast, weighting factor) even for sluggish, heavily smoothed forecasts as in the bottom section of Fig. 24. This also makes the method especially suitable for computers because it makes only modest demands on their storage facilities.

I have described only the simplest principles of automatic forecasting. More sophisticated moving total methods have been evolved which can correct for seasonal and secular trends—a full treatment of the subject would call for a whole book to itself rather than one chapter only. The author has written such a book[1] which is on about the same technical level as this one—it deals in the main with analytical methods. However, synthetic methods have recently been subjected to the scientific attack, no doubt as a result of psychological studies of *consumer motivation* and the analysis in organizational terms of *market structure*. The former is generally restricted to single products like motor-cars, tobacco or cosmetics, but the latter is capable of mathematical expression in more general situations. Together they have led to the concept of a *demand function* as an aid to forecasting.

Demand Functions

Demand functions or *market-generating* forecasts are attempts to put synthetic forecasts on to a more scientific basis and 'scientific' implies here, as it so often does in business affairs, 'mathematical'. This does not, however, preclude a description of its general concepts in everyday language.

Consider, for example, the case of a manufacturer of notepaper who wanted to make a medium-term or long-term forecast of the demand for his product. He began with a few reasonable assumptions about the nature of his customers and about their behaviour. First, they are a constant fraction of the total population—a reasonable assumption because although babies do not use notepaper, parenthood increases its consumption by adults. Secondly, an individual's consumption of notepaper can only increase, decrease or stay constant: it is only necessary to assume that any increase or decrease will be at a steady rate in order to fit any one of these three possibilities to what mathematicians call a *linear function*.[2] At this point the forecaster has the choice of either making his own estimate of the future population or using figures from professional demographers: in the actual case he did the former, assuming that the average rate of growth of population over the previous fifteen years would continue for at least five years more. The final forecast is obtained from the simple equation—

> Forecast of national demand in year n =
> Number of customers in year n × Consumption per head

[1] A. BATTERSBY, *Sales Forecasting* (Cassell, 1969).

[2] See A. BATTERSBY, *Mathematics in Management* (Penguin, 1966), Chapter 3. In the case described here, time is the independent variable and the independent variable is 'consumption of notepaper per customer'.

This almost childishly simple reasoning yields a most impressive formula when the two factors on the right-hand side are replaced by their mathematical expressions: it is also useful as well as elegant.

Consider as a second example the demand for telephone cables or exchanges as distinct from telephones themselves. One possible element in a theory of demand might be that a telephone line links a *pair* of people and so the demand for it may be proportional, not to the population itself but to the *number of pairs* that can be formed from it. In a population of 100, a single member may pair off with any one of the other 99, so the number of possible pairs appears at first to be 100×99; however, when we consider that 'A chooses B' gives the same pair as 'B chooses A', we see that the true number of possible pairs is only half this, that is, 4,950. If the population increases to 120, the number of possible pairs becomes $120 \times 119 \times \frac{1}{2}$ which is 7,140, so an increase of 44 per cent in the forecast would be generated by an increase of only 20 per cent in the population. In practice, the introduction of other factors would 'shade' the number of possible pairs, so the forecast increase in the demand for telephone cable would be less than 44 per cent but still greater than 20 per cent.

Once we have taken the step of considering pairs rather than individuals, we can go on to think in terms of demand being proportional to even bigger groups: unfortunately this wider thinking has been little explored so there is a lack of the practical experience by which the best theories are tested and selected. Furthermore, mathematical procedures which are quite adequate for populations of a hundred or so, present some difficulty when applied to millions.

When on top of this the forecaster tries to use mathematical predictors of human behaviour, he may achieve some tiny measure of success in describing individuals, but as he hops across this unknown swampy territory from tuft to sociological tuft in studying the behaviour of a group, he may easily lose his footing and find himself floundering in a morass of conflicting opinions. He may comfort himself with the consoling thought that for stock control at least, the relatively simple methods of short-term forecasting, called *extrapolation*, are usually quite good enough.

Exercises (see Table XI)

1. If the sales of chocolic acid in the first week of 1971 were 194 tons,

i.e. twice the average for 1970, calculate the new values of the moving average for (*a*) 4 weeks, (*b*) 13 weeks, and (*c*) 52 weeks.

2. Calculate the new exponentially weighted moving totals for factors of (*a*) 0·60, (*b*) 0·86, (*c*) 0·96.

CHAPTER 6

Standard Systems of Stock Control

> ... like a deep well
> That owes two buckets filling one another;
> The emptier ever dancing in the air,
> The other down, unseen and full of water:
>
> SHAKESPEARE, *King Richard II.*

A complete system of stock control must contain at least three sub-systems, which are—

(1) A method of forecasting.
(2) A way of answering the question, "When do we re-order?"
(3) A way of deciding how much to order.
(4) A communications (or information) network.

The first of these was dealt with in the preceding chapter and the last will be deferred until Chapter 10. Items (2) and (3) are usually considered together either as the *two-bin system* (which the Americans call the *(S,s)* system or the *constant cycle* (American *S,t*) system. In the former, re-ordering is determined by the stock level, in the latter it is a function of time.

The Two-Bin System

This system is illustrated by Fig. 26 which shows a simple direct method of stock control. The two bins contain, let us say, mild-steel welding rods. These rods are taken from the first bin as required; as soon as it is empty, more rods are ordered. While awaiting delivery of these, we use the rods in the second bin.

The replenishments arrive just as the second bin becomes empty, so they should be of a quantity sufficient to refill both bins. The period covered by the second bin is, of course, the lead time. As we have seen, this may be either fixed or variable but for the time being we shall consider only the case of a fixed lead time. Such *deterministic* cases are the easiest to deal with theoretically, but probably the rarest in practice.

If the lead time is fixed at 4 weeks and the welding rods are sold or otherwise consumed at a steady rate of one hundred a week, then

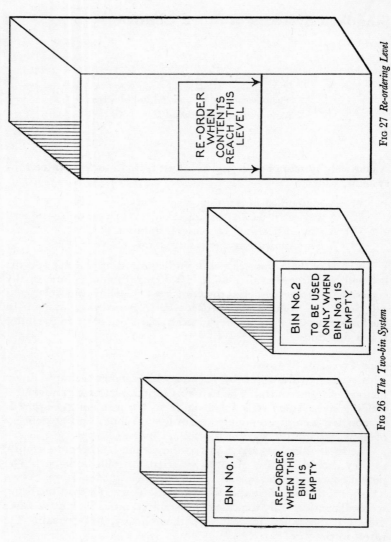

BIN No.1

RE-ORDER
WHEN THIS
BIN IS
EMPTY

BIN No.2

TO BE USED
ONLY WHEN
BIN No.1 IS
EMPTY

FIG 26 *The Two-bin System*

RE-ORDER
WHEN
CONTENTS
REACH THIS
LEVEL

FIG 27 *Re-ordering Level*

the rule for ordering replenishments will be as shown in Fig. 28 and the second bin will have a capacity of 4 × 100, i.e. 400 rods. This figure is called the *Re-ordering Level*, abbreviated to ROL.

It now becomes obvious that two separate bins are not really necessary at all. We can put one on top of the other and mark the re-ordering level as shown in Fig. 27. One very successful system operated by I.C.I. Dyestuffs Division did just this, using the stocks themselves as indicators, but the ROL is more likely to be found as part of a *model* of the stock (*see* page 91) such as a bin card on which changes in stock are logged. Even without this sophistication, I.C.I. Dyestuffs saved in this way more than £20,000 a year, almost evenly divided between physical and mental effort in stores and offices respectively, to offset the once-for-all-cost of installing the system, £30,000.

One simple modification of this method is to add an Advance Re-ordering Level (AROL) or, as it is sometimes called, a Warning

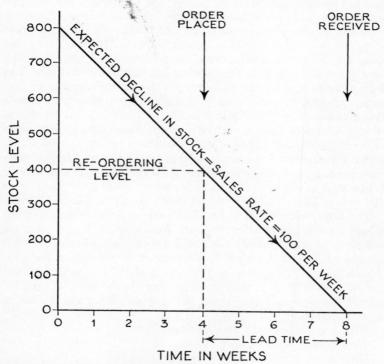

FIG 28 *Graphical Model of Deterministic Two-bin System*

Re-ordering Level (*WROL*). This requires us to set a *warning period* and may be simply illustrated by reference to Fig. 28. Suppose we decide on a warning period of 4 weeks over and above the lead time, the AROL for welding rods will be 800 items. Using an AROL is an antidote to the 'ill-defined levels' discussed at greater length in the section on the constant cycle system which follows this one. It may also have the advantage of sorting out 'stocks which may soon need action' from 'stocks about which we may relax', thereby reducing the work load on the office.

The AROL, if adopted, is a recognition of the fact that the lead time may not be a single constant figure, but one which varies. However, before pursuing the idea of a variable lead time we must first allow consideration of the variable nature of withdrawals (sales), that is, of a *stochastic* system.

Iu practice, the stochastic element in withdrawals from the system makes it necessary for us to set our ROL rather higher than it would be for a perfectly predictable demand. Let us examine the situation more closely in the light of our studies of chocolic acid in Chapter 3.

In Fig. 29 our present stock is 482 tons, and in one week we expect to sell 100 tons of this, leaving us with 382 tons. However, we know from Fig. 13 that our sales could be as high as 141 tons, in which case our stock at the end of the week might be as low as 341 tons. You will remember that the difference between the maximum and expected sales, 41 tons, is our buffer stock; by applying the simple rule given on page 49 we find the buffer stocks for 2, 3 and 4 weeks to be 58, 72 and 82 tons respectively. These correspond to maximum sales of 258, 372 and 482 tons, and to the lower curved line in Fig. 29, which traces out the maximum sales or minimum stocks. The complete set of figures is given in Table X. If the lead time for chocolic acid is four weeks, then our ROL is obviously 482 tons, made up of 400 tons of expected sales and 82 tons of buffer stock.

The upper curved line in Fig. 29 shows what the decline in stock would be if *minimum* sales occurred. You may remember that we originally took a probability level of 2 per cent, therefore the shaded area between the two curved lines represents 96 per cent probability. That is to say, if we allowed an initial stock of 482 tons to be depleted for four weeks by randomly varying sales of chocolic acid and repeated this over and over again, the graph showing the decline of stock would be—

Inside the shaded area 96 times out of every 100;
Above it twice out of every 100 times;
Below it twice out of every 100 times.

This shows in a slightly different way what we have already said

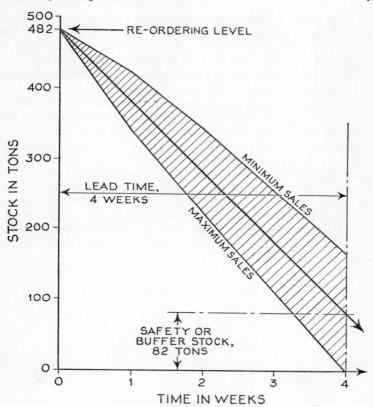

FIG 29 *Graphical Model of Stochastic Two-bin System*

in Chapter 4—that a buffer stock of 82 tons will save us from running out of stock on all but two out of every hundred occasions.

In the two-bin system, the concepts of Re-ordering Level (ROL) and Re-ordering Quantity (ROQ) replace those of Minimum and Maximum Stocks in less precise systems. How are these ideas related? The Minimum Stock is now a variable quantity, but its average value is equal to the buffer stock (although in some cases the so-called "Minimum Stock" is really the ROL). The Maximum Stock is found by adding the ROQ to the buffer stock. The Average Stock lies half-way between the Maximum and Minimum Stocks and is equal to the buffer stock plus half the ROQ.

The perspicacious reader may raise an objection at this point and say that for working out economic lot sizes in Chapter 2 we assumed

the buffer stock to be zero. Since this assumption is no longer valid,
are we still justified in using the method given in Chapter 2? Yes,
we are. The buffer stock gives rise to an additional stockholding cost
of £0·06 a week but this is added equally to each row of costs in
Table I. Therefore it does not affect the lot size for which the total
cost is at a minimum, although the total cost itself is increased. (It is
now no longer true that the ordering and stockholding costs are
equal at the economic lot size, although their sum is still a minimum.)

The figures for chocolic acid are such that its ROL and ROQ are
approximately equal; this makes it rather a special case. What happens if the ROL is much greater than the ROQ? We then have a
situation as shown in Fig. 30; the ROL remains at 482 tons but the
ROQ is now only 100 tons. The actual stock in hand never rises
above the ROL, yet obviously orders must be placed somehow. In
practice, we have to treat all outstanding orders as though they were
already in stock—in other words, we must add the 'stock in transit'
(i.e. orders outstanding) to the 'stock in hand' before comparing the
total stock with the ROL.

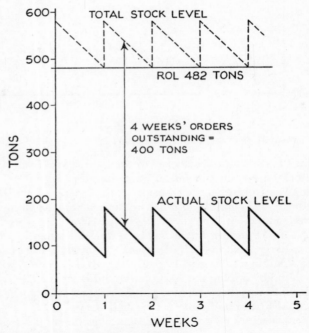

FIG 30 *Two-bin System with ROQ less than ROL*

We have a more conventional situation when the ROQ is greater than the ROL. With the latter still set at 482 tons, let us imagine our ROQ to be 800 tons. The re-ordering pattern would appear as in Fig. 31. We now have to consider an interesting point about our 2 per cent risk level: this risk is being incurred only during the lead time when an order is outstanding. During the four weeks immediately after an order has been received there is virtually no risk. The *average* risk level is only 1 per cent.

We cannot go very deeply into these complications within the limited scope of this book; it is almost impossible to do so without

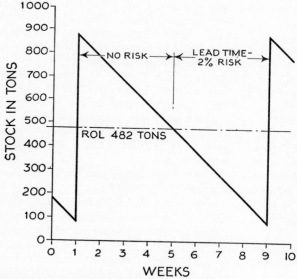

FIG 31 *Two-bin System with ROQ greater than ROL*

delving into statistical theory. They are mentioned as one more example of the care which must be exercised when a practical system is drawn up.

Strictly speaking, we are now in a position to set up a two-bin system of stock control, but with one important restriction. So far we have assumed that average sales would remain constant (apart from random variations), but we must be able to cope with sales for which the average value may also change unpredictably. This brings up the problem of sales forecasting which was discussed in Chapter 5. In view of the importance which that chapter attached to the

4

assumptions on which a forecast is made, let us list them here explicitly. We assume—

(1) Either there is no secular (i.e. long-term) trend or it is so small as to be negligible;

(2) Either there is no seasonal or periodic trend, or it is very small, or its period is thirteen weeks;

(3) The random fluctuations are adequately smoothed by averaging over thirteen observations.

On this basis we choose an unweighted Moving Quarterly Average (M.Q.A., column (6) in Fig. 32).

We now have our complete system, which can be specified by a set of rules. The calculations can conveniently be summarized on the Stock Control Form (Fig. 32), and a specimen set of figures is shown. We assume that we are at the beginning of 1971: Table V (page 34) gives us the sales figures for the previous quarter, which we enter in column (4); it also gives us the Moving Quarterly Total—that is, the sum of the previous 13 weeks' sales (1,309 tons) which we enter in column (5). Dividing this by 13 gives the Moving Quarterly Average (101 tons) which goes into column (6)—this is the sales forecast. Suppose we have an initial stock of 500 tons in hand— column (7)—and none on order. Our ROL is 482 tons, so there is no need to place an order.

We now enter Week 1: no goods are received. The sales for this week are 76 tons, so our new MQT will be $(1,309 + 76 - 131)$ tons, i.e. 1,254 tons; the corresponding MQA is 96 tons. The stock in hand falls to 424 tons; nothing is on order, so our total stock is also 424 tons. This is less than the ROL, so we must place another order. What is the ROQ?

The relevant costs and rate of interest for chocolic acid were given in Chapter 2 (pages 20–22), and we worked out an economic batch size (ROQ) of 400 tons, for a sales rate of 100 tons a week. For a sales rate of 96 tons a week, the ROQ is rather less, being in fact 392 tons. There is no need to go through the entire calculation on page 23 every time; if all the figures remain fixed except the sales, we can find quite easily that the ROQ is equal to the square root of the (forecast) sales multiplied by 40 and use either this factor or the conversion scale in Fig. 8.

Changes in the size of the ROQ are a very significant feature of the two-bin system. Let us look for a moment at the sales in recent weeks: we have sold 110 tons in each of the last two weeks, but now sales have fallen to 76 tons. (By way of simplification, we are ignoring any effects that the Christmas season may have had on the sales.) Is

STOCK CONTROL FORM
(TWO-BIN SYSTEM)

WEEK NO.	GOODS RECEIVED TONS	SALES, TONS				STOCKS, TONS			ORDER PLACED	NOTES
		THIS WEEK	LAST QUARTER	M.Q.T.	M.Q.A.	IN HAND	ON ORDER	TOTAL		
(1)	(2)	(3)	(4)	(5)	(6)	(7)	(8)	(9)	(11)	
0	0	76	131	1309	101	500	0	·500		ROL = 482 tons (12)
1			125	1254	96	424	0	424	392	To obtain the ROQ, multiply the square root of (6) by 40.
2			92							
3			141							
4			70							
5	392		113							
6			69							
7			122							
8			88							
9			56							
10			82							
11			110							
12			110							
13										

FIG 32 Stock Control Form

this merely a random fluctuation or is it the beginning of a downward trend? We just do not know, so perhaps our natural human reaction would be to compromise and wait to see how next week's sales turn out.

Now see how the system has behaved. By averaging sales over the last thirteen weeks instead of merely looking at week-to-week figures, it has smoothed out the fall from 34 tons (110 − 76) to only 5 tons (101 − 96). This small change is reflected in the slight reduction of the ROQ to 392 tons: we have gone a little way towards anticipating a fall in sales but without making the large 'panic' changes which so often throw stocks into complete disorder.

You may find it interesting to continue this exercise using the sets of sales figures in Table XII. Of these, set B corresponds to a continuation of sales at their current level; set A corresponds to a sudden and sustained decrease of 20 tons a week in the second week, and set C to a similar increase of 20 tons a week.

TABLE XII: *Alternative sets of sales figures for chocolic acid in the first quarter of 1971*

Week No.	Weekly Sales, tons		
	A	B	C
1	76	76	76
2	62	78	157
3	65	110	119
4	85	87	126
5	71	100	170
6	71	102	128
7	73	81	160
8	76	108	151
9	90	84	96
10	91	127	146
11	83	114	126
12	62	98	145
13	103	115	86

The decreased demand of set A causes orders both to diminish in size and to become less frequent; this change occurs gradually over thirteen weeks and then settles down to the new conditions unless other disturbances occur. The system will work well at the new level of sales, but the ROL may be rather too high if the standard deviation has fallen along with the mean, as often happens. This would mean that our buffer stock would be covering a lower risk level than it was designed for originally. Obviously we need to recalculate the ROL from time to time as a routine check, but especially so when the average sales are seen to have changed.

Set C causes a change in the opposite direction; orders increase in size and become more frequent, while the risk of being out of stock may increase slightly.

A two-bin stock system, then, is able to adjust itself to conditions other than those for which it was planned, and this capacity for self-adjustment is a necessary part of *any* practical control system. Its importance with respect to forecasting was discussed in Chapter 5. We may also note in passing that a two-bin system *can* be used even when the lead time has a stochastic variation. The principle which is followed in setting buffer stocks is that they are derived from the *standard deviation of sales during the lead time*. This principle is identical with that used for a fixed lead time. It may be applied directly by keeping a record of withdrawals during the lead time and then finding their standard deviation either by plotting a graph on probability paper or calculating it statistically. However, it is possible to use the sales measured over regular accounting periods in conjunction with records of the variations in lead or delivery times,[1] as Chapter 9 will show.

We shall now look briefly at an alternative to the two-bin system.

The Constant Cycle System

The constant cycle system, like the two-bin system, sets out to answer two questions about re-ordering. The first is "When?" and the second, "How much?" The answer to the first of these is decided by considering the *time* instead of the stock *level*. Orders are placed at constant intervals of time, which will usually be chosen for convenience in administration—perhaps one week, one month or three months. The best period may be found by a minimum-cost procedure similar to that described in Chapter 2, that is, by minimizing the total costs of ordering and stockholding. Once the time interval has been decided in this way, it cannot be varied without disturbing the organization. For example, we may have decided that our stock of split pins should be reviewed once a week, say on Monday morning. We should probably not change the cycle, because in doing so we should lose the advantage of *regularity*. Thus, the small adjustments in ROQ which were permitted under the two-bin system have no counterparts in the constant cycle system as applied in practice.

The second question, "How much?" may be answered in three ways—

[1] And how they can vary! A survey by Yale & Towne Ltd. showed that 28 per cent of their suppliers took twice as long as they promised, with 81 per cent failing by one-quarter or more.

(1) Enough to restore the stock to some predetermined level.

(2) Enough to meet the sales forecast during the next interval.

(3) Enough to meet the sales forecast and simultaneously adjust the stock.

We shall assume to begin with that the second of these rules is to be used with a buffer stock to absorb random fluctuations in sales, as in the two-bin system.

At this point, we need to digress for a moment and consider exactly what is contained in the 'lead time'. We originally defined it (page 49) as the time interval between deciding to place an order and receiving the order. With either system we make our decision when we review the stock position; with the two-bin system we are supposed to do this continuously. In practice we could hardly be expected to do so except in special cases (automatic distant-reading gauges on oil tanks, for instance), and the stock is inspected at intervals. Such intervals may be regular or irregular, but will generally be short; if they are not, extra stock must be carried to allow for them.

Take the two-bin example given in the last section: we examine our stock of chocolic acid one Monday morning and find it to be 500 tons. This is above the ROL of 482 tons, so we do not place an order—or do we? May we not argue, "The stock is only 18 tons above the ROL and we shall probably not look at it again before next Monday; the stock will certainly fall below the ROL long before then, so perhaps we had better order now?" Our 500 tons is no longer being compared with 482 tons, but with some ill-defined level which allows for roughly an extra week's sales-plus-uncertainty, and is higher than the official ROL. Unofficial adjustments of this sort undermine and may eventually destroy a control system: they tend to become more and more generous, and so excess stocks begin to accumulate. It is better to recognize this need and allow for it in the first place by including the review period in the lead time in addition to the normal delivery period. The four weeks' lead time in our last example contained three weeks' delivery period and an allowance of one week for review.

Now in the constant cycle system, this review period will be the re-ordering interval, the economic value of which is four weeks (equivalent to a ROQ of 400 tons). The total lead time is the sum of this and the three weeks' delivery time, making seven weeks. The buffer stock is found by the rule on page 49 to be 109 tons—this is 27 tons greater than the 82 tons which we calculated for the two-bin system. Theoretical studies have shown that the average stock in a

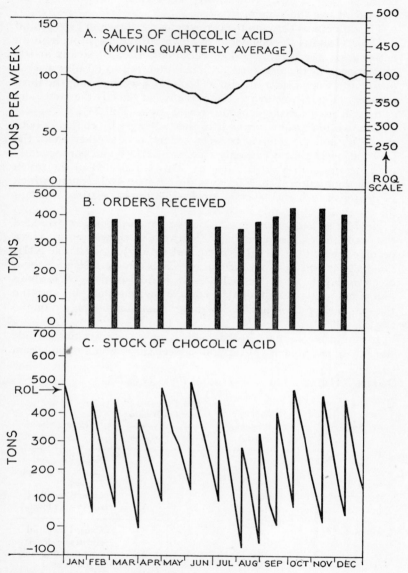

FIG 33 *Comparison of Systems (I) Two-bin*

constant cycle system will always be greater than that in an equivalent two-bin system.

The differences between the two systems are shown in Figs. 33 and 34. Fig. 33 shows the behaviour of a two-bin system throughout an entire year; apart from random variations, sales are steady at 100 tons a week in the first quarter. They then fall to 80 tons a week during the second quarter, rise to 120 tons a week during the third quarter and finally return to 100 tons a week. Exactly the same sales pattern is used for the constant cycle system (Fig. 34).

The two-bin system responds to these changes by changing both the ROQ and the interval between orders; on the other hand, the constant cycle system can only change its ROQ and consequently needs to do so to a greater degree. This is reflected in the much greater fluctuation in stock levels in the constant cycle system, which in turn gives a higher average stock—298 tons as against 248 tons for the two-bin system.

Now let us look at those occasions on which the orders exceeded the available stock, so a backlog or 'negative stock' was set up. These occurred three times in each system and are analysed in Table XIII. On balance, the two-bin system gave a better performance for a given outlay on stock. Nevertheless, its administrative cost is about four times as high as that of the constant cycle system, because the two-bin method demands weekly rather than monthly checks on the stock level.

It should be emphasized that both systems were working outside their designed capacity of 100 tons a week. Provision for changes in

TABLE XIII: *Analysis of backlogs in Figs. 33 and 34*

System	Week in which backlog occurred	Amount of Backlog		Comments
		Tons	Days	
Two-bin	13	4	$\frac{1}{25}$	Negligible, and part of the accepted 2% risk.
	31	73	$\frac{3}{4}$ }	Caused by rapid rise in sales level.
	34	53	$\frac{1}{2}$	
Constant Cycle	36	72	$\frac{2}{3}$ }	Caused by rapid rise in sales level: note that the backlogs occurred rather later than in two-bin system.
	40	81	$\frac{3}{4}$	
	44	26	$\frac{1}{4}$	

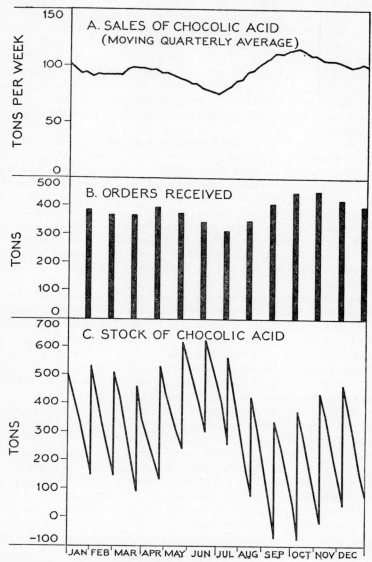

FIG 34 *Comparison of Systems (II) Constant Cycle*

the level of sales can be built into the system, but of course they will make it more complicated. One simpler way, however, would be to recalculate the standard deviation at the end of the year on the assumption that all the variations in sales were due to random effects; this would give protection against future changes in sales of the same general magnitude. This is only a very approximate method; it would not be approved by most statisticians because it ignores 'autocorrelation', or the tendency of one high weekly sales figure to be followed by another high figure more often than not, or a low one by another low one. Autocorrelation is, again, beyond the scope of this book.

The constant cycle system loses some of its sluggishness if we design it not only to meet the expected sales but also to apply a stock correction which depends on the difference between the measured stock and a target stock (Method 3 on page 86). Some rule-of-thumb methods fall into this category, which is unfortunate because such systems can become very unstable in some conditions. Their unsatisfactory performance in practice then leads to a lack of confidence in stock control generally. Such hasty judgments are unfair—would you condemn all springs just because your own car rolled badly on corners? The fault lies not in the theory, but in its imperfect application.

An unstable stock system is one which creates within itself the very disturbances which it should suppress; these disturbances usually take the form of severe oscillations in the level of stock. Two of the factors which cause instability are *over-correction* and *delay*.

Over-correction is illustrated in Fig. 35. The control system which it illustrates is practically the same as that shown in Fig. 34, although the pattern of sales is different. The lead time is four weeks and the sales rate remains at a steady 100 tons a week, apart from random fluctuations. We place an order every four weeks and the re-ordering rule is: "Replace the sales during the previous four weeks and add a quantity sufficient to restore the stock in hand to 500 tons." For example, at the end of Week 4 the sales for the previous four weeks had been 351 tons; the stock in hand was 549 tons, so 49 tons must be subtracted in order to restore the stock to the target value of 500 tons. We order $(351 - 49)$ tons, i.e. 302 tons.

This is obviously a case of over-correction; we are compensating for the below-average sales *directly* by replacing only 351 tons, and again *indirectly* because the increased stock is also an outcome of the lower sales.

The oscillation which ensues is seen most clearly in the 'Goods Received' section of Fig. 35. The re-ordering quantities obviously reflect the random fluctuations in sales and even amplify them. However, the system does not get out of hand, and can have advantages when we want a rapid response to real changes in the level of sales.

When stock adjustments are fed back in this way, it is generally advisable to 'damp' their effects by making only a fraction of the total adjustment. Thus in a similar system with a damping factor of one-half, the quantity ordered at the end of Week 4 would have been (351 — 24) tons, i.e. 327 tons.

Fig. 36 shows the same system but with the lead time increased to five weeks. The re-ordering rule is the same as before, except that the target stock now has to be 100 tons, because it is measured at a different point in the time cycle. The increased lead time (five weeks) is now greater than the review period (four weeks), so any adjustment made in, say, Week 4 will not take effect until Week 9. Meanwhile, another adjustment is made in Week 8 *before* the first one has had time to take effect. This *delay* is equivalent to over-correcting still further, and we see the disastrous effect in Fig. 36. The oscillations which are set up go on increasing and the system soon becomes completely unmanageable.

We can easily restore some measure of stability to this system by adjusting not just the stock in hand but the total stock in hand and on order, as recommended on pages 79 and 80. This would have the effect of applying the adjustment made in Week 4 immediately instead of having to wait until Week 9. The system would then behave in much the same way as is shown in Fig. 35.

As a matter of interest, we show in Fig. 37 how the control system of Fig. 35 responds to the varying sales used for Fig. 33 and 34. The changes in the rate of sales cause fluctuations in the ordering and stock levels which are quite violent, but not uncontrollably so.

The theory of feedback control circuits was originally worked out for use in electrical engineering, and whether its mathematics are regarded as simple or complicated depends upon the point of view of the manager. Briefly, the theory demands that a dynamic model of the system be set up. In this context, the adjective 'dynamic' is used in contrast to the word 'static'; that is to say, it describes changes which occur with respect to time. The model will generally be an equation containing differential coefficients of the first and second order. Thus sales may be expressed as a rate of change of stock level with time (first order) and allowing for the rate of change of sales brings in the coefficients of the second order. Such methods are undoubtedly powerful but, as ever, in using them one risks using a mathematical steam-hammer to crack a managerial nut.

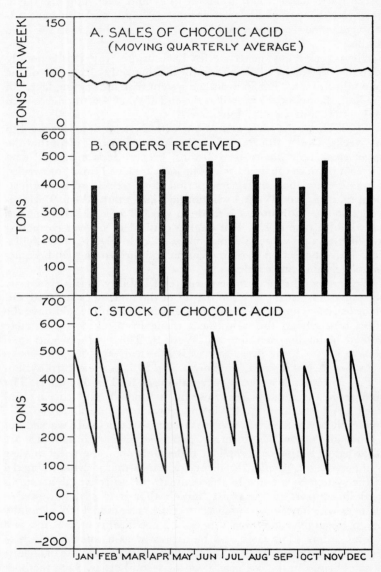

FIG 35 *Constant Cycle System with Target Stock Adjustment (i) 4 Weeks' Lead Time*

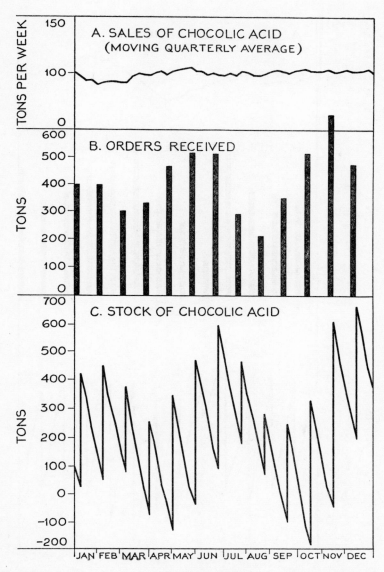

Fig 36 *Constant Cycle System with Target Stock Adjustment (ii) 5 Weeks' Lead Time*

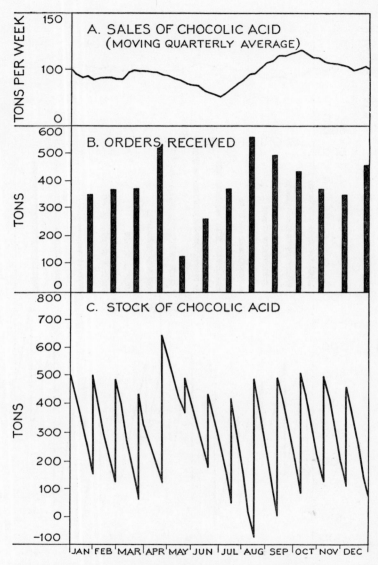

FIG 37 *Constant Cycle System with Target Stock Adjustment* (*As Fig. 35 but with varying average sales*)

Mixed Systems

There is no limit to the number of possible systems, since the operating rules may be built up from combinations of the universal principles described in this book. Some more special ones, are, naturally enough, matters for the specialist rather than the general manager.

Think, for instance, of the 'two-bin' system: strictly interpreted, it requires that the storekeeper keep a continuous watch on stock levels, night and day, until the ROL is just reached; as I have expounded it for the sake of simplicity, it contains the assumption that the stock is depleted by infinitesimally small units. In practice, withdrawals may be in sizeable chunks so the stock level falls in a series of steps; even though they may be small, several can accumulate between checks because the storekeeper may check a stock level only once a day. Compared with the intervals between orders of course, this is short enough to be virtually the same as a continuous watch. Even so, it still introduces a 'constant cycle' element. Again, it is hard to believe that a manager of stocks, faced with a disastrous deficiency, would refuse to take action because the rules say he may not order until the first of next month.

It follows that 'ready-made' systems will not always suit a company's requirements, either local or general, and even my most computer-addicted colleagues agree that an otherwise completely automatic stock control system will be all the better for an admixture of human skill and judgment.

The Free Stock System

The so-called 'free stock' is calculated by deducting the orders in hand from the current stock level and orders are placed when the free stock falls to zero. It has some merits and may be recommended as a *supplement* to a more modern system such as the two-bin or constant cycle, but is not very good when used on its own. Its great drawback is over-caution, because in effect it forecasts the withdrawals from stock without taking corresponding replenishments into account; moreover, it forecasts over an ill-defined period which depends on the haphazard arrival of orders. Suppose, for example, that one of the orders is for 100 tons of chocolic acid for delivery six months hence. The free stock system would require that this 100 tons be held immobile for six months, when it might be 'earning its keep' as an extra buffer. Strategic stocks often fall into this category —even a relatively inert substance like aviation spirit can deteriorate when kept static for years. In fact, the free stock system is yet another example of a general rule: 'excessive caution leads to excessive stock'.

96 *A Guide to Stock Control*

Multi-stage Stock Systems

Multi-stage systems are appropriate if a stock of raw materials plus a 'stock' of processing capacity are considered equivalent to a stock of finished product. They are a new idea, so not much practical experience is available; one way of attacking a multi-stage problem is to draw a *complete* flow process chart similar to Fig. 56 but extending all the way from the main stock or stocks of raw material to that of the finished product. Such a chart may well be transformed into an arrow diagram, because it must be quantified by having process durations entered on it. The detailed construction of the multi-stage stock system is then very much an individual matter and may be based on a network analysis of the arrow diagram.[1] One of the attractions of a multi-stage system is that it offers an additional method of smoothing seasonal fluctuations by 'swinging' the stock from product to raw material and back according to the timing of the seasonal peak.

Exercise

1. Sales of Jekaldehyde show a monthly average of 60 tons with a standard deviation of 15 tons. The lead time is 9 months. Design a two-bin system for Jekaldehyde.

[1] A. BATTERSBY, *Network Analysis for Planning and Scheduling* (Macmillan, 3rd Edition, 1970) page 216.

CHAPTER 7

Problems of Variety

> ... through mazes running;
> Untwisting all the chains that tie
> The hidden soul of harmony.
>
> MILTON, *L'Allegro.*

As we saw in earlier chapters, most of the basic theory of stock control is concerned with the behaviour of a single stock centre but as we have also seen, such individual centres cannot always be isolated neatly. They will frequently interact with each other to cause the overlap between stock and production control which is discussed in terms of a simple case, three interacting products, on pages 163 to 168; the stocks in this example depend upon each other because they have one thing in common: they are all linked to the same production process. So if we regard the single stock centre as a *point*, a variety of products dependent on one process or machine may be thought of as a *line*; in mathematicians' language, we can say that the problem has gained one dimension. This typifies the situation in a warehouse (Fig. 39), the 'process' being the simple operations of handling and storage, breaking down into smaller lots and so on. From this simple case we progress naturally to the situation illustrated in Fig. 1, where the vertical dimension, variety of products alone, is augmented by a horizontal dimension—variety of *processes*: boiling, chipping, milling, stamping, wrapping and packing.

A two-dimensional problem like this, represented by the square in Fig. 38, may be dealt with by treating stock and production control as an integrated problem, and the family of methods called 'mathematical programming' will often yield a suitable model for solving it.[1] The manager wishing to employ mathematical programming on his inventory problems will be obliged to do two things.

First, he will have to say clearly what his objective is—and 'clearly'

---

[1] The simplest member of this family is called Linear Programming: to explain it adequately in detail requires a mathematical treatment. Those interested in such a description are referred to Chapters 4, 5 and 6 of the author's book *Mathematics in Management* (3rd imp., Penguin 1970).

means that the objective must ultimately be laid down in a mathematical equation called the 'objective function' or 'control function'. *Secondly*, he will have to define a set of *constraints* or *restrictions* which impose limits on the problem. Some of these will be simple and obvious, like "no stock level can be lower than zero"; others will be harder, like "the total of all stocks of such-and-such a type must not exceed the capacity of the store". (I know of a case in which this restriction was apparently exceeded. A bright young man, puzzling over a discrepancy, calculated the physical volume of stock in a provincial storage depot as exceeding the total cubic capacity of that depot, thereby uncovering a fraud.) A set of such statements, expressed numerically in suitable form, can be processed by a standard procedure, with the help of an efficient computer if desired, to yield an 'optimum' (usually least-cost) solution which will include appropriate stock levels. The calculations of Appendix 2 are a simple type of mathematical programming.

Finally, the processes themselves demand stocks—they are performed by men who draw tools from a store, or by machines which also demand spare parts, tools such as cups and dies, lubricants, abrasives, and so on. This we can consider as the 'third dimension' through which our stocks must extend. Stocks of this type are dealt with in Chapter 8.

The total inventory of stocks in a factory may run to tens of thousands of items, and one often hears the despairing cry, "But how can we *hope* to control so many stocks?" The immediate answer to this is a simple one—the stocks are in fact being controlled somehow or other at this moment, even though it may well take a major disorganization of the factory's activities to draw attention to a shortage or a surplus. The question is not whether the control exists, but whether it is adequate. This in turn may be broken down into two other questions—

(1) Are the existing staff controlling stocks in the most efficient way?

(2) Are we providing sufficient staff to exert adequate control on our stocks?

To the extent that question 2 is one of management, it is dealt with in Chapter 10. It may also be tackled objectively if we ask—

(1) What would be the cost of adding an extra member to the staff (or the saving achieved by removing one)?

(2) What benefit, in terms of reduced operating costs, would result from doing so?

Appendix 2 gives an example of this approach.

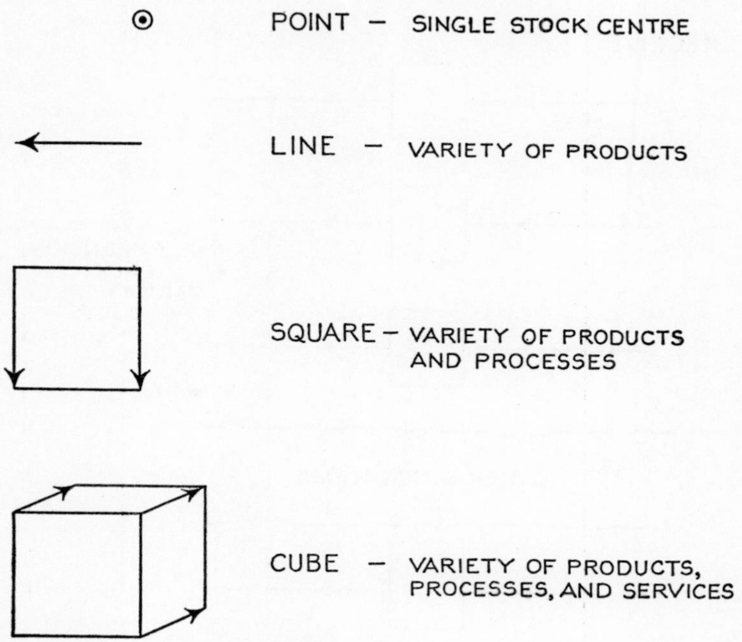

POINT — SINGLE STOCK CENTRE

LINE — VARIETY OF PRODUCTS

SQUARE — VARIETY OF PRODUCTS
AND PROCESSES

CUBE — VARIETY OF PRODUCTS,
PROCESSES, AND SERVICES

FIG 38 *The Three Dimensions of Inventories*

The question of efficient working will also arise. In a store containing thousands of items, the number of staff required to do a complete analysis for each individual item would be prohibitively high. There is a system which classifies stocks into categories (usually three) for treatment by complete analysis (A), rough analysis (B), and very rough analysis (C). It is sometimes called the 'ABC system', for obvious reasons and sometimes the Pareto system. The last name is that of a German economist who worked out the distribution of incomes in East Prussia and found that about 20 per cent of the people got 80 per cent of the money. The complete mathematical picture of the distribution is called 'Pareto's Law'. It has been used in many contexts outside welfare economics, including inventories. When applied to the latter, Pareto's Law takes the form, 'Twenty per cent of the items account for eighty per cent of the stock', and this provides a good starting point. Arrange the stock items in order of their values and find a more precise rule for your own business— the result will be a diagram like Fig. 40, which covers five hundred items. It is obviously sensible to allocate the efforts of the staff in

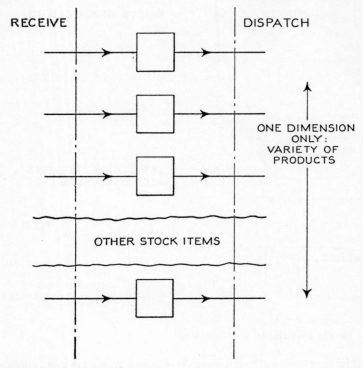

FIG 39 *Stocks in a Warehouse*

the same proportions, so that four-fifths of their time is spent on the first hundred items of stock (A) and one-fifth on (B) and (C). You will also identify in this way the few items which will repay a fairly close analysis of demand or supply as described in Chapter 3, those for which the rapid methods of Chapter 5 are more appropriate, and finally the large number of items which can continue under the present arbitrary control figures, at least for the time being.

Stocks can also be classified as 'fast-moving' and 'slow-moving', and this second classification is a valuable supplement to the one described above. First calculate the 'residence time' for each stock item by dividing the average number of units held in stock by the number of units sold in a year (or consumed, whichever is appropriate). With an average stock of 200 tons and annual sales of 1,200 tons, the residence time is 2 months. The more commonly used 'turnover' is 6 times a year, which is the reciprocal of the residence

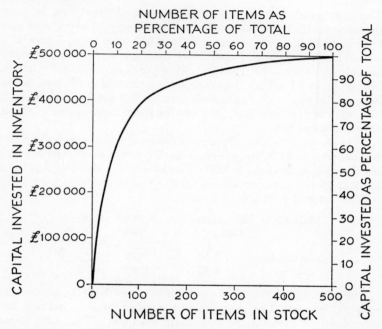

NUMBER OF ITEMS AS
PERCENTAGE OF TOTAL

FIG 40 *Capital Invested in Inventory Against Number of Stock Items*

time. I prefer to use 'residence time' because it is easier to equate mentally with 'fast-moving'. I have also deliberately chosen 'number of units' rather than 'value', because the cost per item is irrelevant: it appears in both numerator and denominator and cancels out.

Arrange the stock items in order of decreasing residence time and compare the list with the 'investment-versus-items' list. The two should show some agreement: the main raw materials and finished products should tend to combine high investment with short residence time. At the other end of the scale, spare parts should be in the low-value, long-residence class. Any items which are badly out of line would be selected for investigation in detail individually if their value or cost appeared to justify it. The case of the Duddie-Coost Company which follows, shows how it may even pay to reduce the margin of profit on an item in order to reduce its stock-holding cost.

The Duddie-Coost Case
The Duddie-Coost Co. Ltd. manufactures two grades of Sark-Links.

The first grade is guaranteed to withstand two tons without breaking and is the main product—10,000 are sold every year and individual orders range from 100 to 4,000 at a time. There is a second grade, guaranteed to withstand only one ton: it was originally brought in as a means of getting rid of the occasional faulty batch, but the process has been improved and the second grade now has to be specially made. Only one customer for this grade now remains: his orders arrive irregularly, but one for 2,000 items comes in about once every two years.

In order to avoid disturbances to the production programme the company keeps 2,000 second-grade Sark-Links in stock. The average stock of first-grade links is 5,000. The cost of stockholding has been fixed at 25 per cent per annum by the Board.

The cost and selling prices are—

Sark-Links	Manufacturing Cost per Unit	Selling Price	Profit
	£	£	£
1st Grade	0·50	0·75	0·25
2nd Grade	0·40	0·60	0·20

The stock of 2,000 second-grade links is worth £800, equivalent to £200 a year. The management decided to stop making the second grade and supply the single customer (Tam O'Shanter Ltd., of course) at the same low price from the stock of first-grade links. The Materials Control office calculated that the increase in the first-grade stock would have to be 200 items to preserve the same risk level as before. These are worth £100, so the stockholding cost will go up by £25 a year. The overall saving on stock would be £(200–25) i.e. £175 a year.

The loss of profit would be £0·10 per item, which at 1,000 items a year would be £100 a year. The net saving to the company through pursuing this policy is £75 a year.

(*Note*. The profit on the sale of 1,000 second-grade links a year is £200; all of this is absorbed in holding stock, so the company would not lose even if they were to forgo Tam O'Shanter's business entirely.)

This case is, of course, imaginary, but it is based upon a real example. There are obvious dangers in such behaviour because customers for first-grade links might find out that they could now get the same item at a lower price, so once again we see that the art of managing stocks cannot be divorced from other managerial skills.

Here we have one of the more expensive methods of reducing the variety of products; it is, of course, even better to prevent it from occurring in the first place. Second-grade Sark-Links were the offspring of poor quality control and it would have been better to get rid of the faulty batch as a once-for-all transaction by scrapping or even, if necessary, giving it away. As it was, all the procedures needed to maintain a new stock item were evoked because of a single processing error. This latter is by no means the only cause—there are other offenders, sometimes in the Design Department or its close relative, the Drawing office.

One way of keeping down the number of stock items is by careful design. The connexion with stock control may not be immediately obvious, but it is true that skill in design can save money in the stores. The designer *creates* new items for stock; the fewer he creates, the more money he saves. For instance, he designs a bracket which is secured by a $\frac{1}{2}'' \times 2''$ bolt. A $2\frac{1}{4}''$ bolt would do the job just as well, and is already held as a stock item. In such a case, the slight extra cost of the $2\frac{1}{4}''$ bolt is probably less than the administrative, housing and capital costs which a new stock of $2''$ bolts would incur. This problem, like so many others in industry, is essentially one of communication—of letting the designer know what stock items are already available, classified according to their engineering functions.

Another multiplier of stock items is the non-standard product. A manufacturer produces a single costly machine—a large crane, perhaps—to a unique design. Naturally, the selling price reflects the increased cost of the special design, but does it always include the cost to the manufacturer of keeping spares available? They must be held in stock, or specially made, throughout the useful life of the machine and are useless for any other purpose.

There is also the over-enthusiastic salesman who offers to provide non-standard varieties of his company's products. Each variety has the effect of creating a new stock and eventually a new manu-facturing line—a state of affairs which is not helped by the fact that the new variety does not officially exist. By all means give the customer what he wants, but if what he wants is non-standard, he should pay *all* the extra cost of its production. Too often the administrative and stock-holding costs are lost in the amorphous mass of 'General Overhead Expenses' and not passed on as they should be.

Let us suppose that we have examined all our stocks in this way and turn to the problem of controlling a larger group of, say, a thousand stock items. Can we say that this is simply the problem of the single stock multiplied by one thousand? Alas, we cannot. We have already seen in Chapter 2 how products can interfere with

each other and cause theories which suffice for one stock to be inadequate when applied to many. The interference was a symptom
of having several products *compete* for a single plant. The complete
inventory of stocks shows this competition on a larger scale in two
ways.

First, the separate stocks compete with each other for the resources
devoted to inventory—chiefly working capital, storage space, labour,
and administration.

Secondly, the inventory of stocks competes with other con-
tenders for its share of the total resources of the business. This
second aspect, which is often overlooked, can profoundly affect the
first. Suppose a materials controller were to analyse each separate
stock objectively, using the technique of minimizing cost as described in the previous chapters. The result shows that the total
capital which should be invested in inventory is £5 million against
a present total of £3 million. This is put up to the board as a recommendation to invest the extra £2 million. They are impressed by
the cold logic of the argument, sympathetic to the proposal and
polite to its sponsor—but they just cannot spare the money.

What does the materials controller do now? He sees two things
quite clearly—(1) he ought to have £5 million; (2) he actually has
£3 million. What he will almost certainly decide is to make the best
of a bad job. He will reduce his stocks so that they remain
balanced—that is to say, so that the risk level or the return on
capital is increased uniformly over all. This is still a sort of cost
minimization, but within the limits of a specified total. Minimization of cost takes second place to allocation of resources.

I have suggested that the term Inventory Control be applied to
the strategic aspect, that is, the allocation of total resources to the
entire inventory of stocks and its control as a whole. The title Stock
Control could then be reserved for the problems of individual stock
centres. Using the word 'inventory' in this way is consistent with its
dictionary definition as a *list*; unfortunately, the two words have
become practically interchangeable in common technical usage.

Inventory Control must deal with the productivity of the entire
system of stocks. 'Productivity' means the ratio of what we get out
of something to what we put into it and is analogous to the
engineer's idea of efficiency. We can set out with some precision
what we put into an inventory system, but are we quite sure what
we get out of it? We have already seen that the concepts of protection against risk and minimization of cost may not be entirely
adequate when considered on the large scale—what can we substitute for them? The effect of stocks on a network of processes was

described in Chapter 1 as lubrication; we cannot measure the productivity of a lubricant, although in theory perhaps we could balance its cost against a reduction in wear and consequent breakdown. The analogy with Inventory Control is obvious except that in inventories, as the Duddi-Coost case showed, we are beginning to see ways of estimating the cost of disorganization and hence the value of rationalization. For instance, the chairman of the Tap and Die Corporation estimated in 1962 that if Britain and America could agree to accept the International Standard Screw Thread, his group would save, on stocks alone, "anything up to £200,000 a year".

Grouping and Synchronizing Production

If parts are to come together in a sub-assembly, stocks of work in progress may accumulate if groups of parts are kept waiting for those needed to make up a complete set. Skilful scheduling of production can ensure that the components of the sub-assembly are manufactured in parallel and come together at the right time. Such considerations may override the conventional minimization of cost in producing individual parts and cause total sequences to be planned as shown in Appendix 4. The arithmetic of such a procedure is only very slightly more complicated than that for the single batch, and much may be accomplished with the aid of simple charting techniques like 'Line-of-Balance' (LOB) or its more sophisticated descendant, Network Analysis.[1] The latter is more generally used for one-off or few-off assemblies, but its methods also hold out hope for the man whose problem is one of continuous or semi-continuous (batch) production.

One method of developing such systems is to use a 'simulation' procedure, in other words, to work out the consequences of various policies by trying them out on models (*see* page 91). Such models may require no more than pencil and paper but may with advantage be run on computer. They are sometimes referred to as 'manufacturing rota' systems.

---

[1] The reader interested in acquiring a knowledge of this important latter technique should read K. C. LOCKYER, *Introduction to Critical Path Analysis* (Pitman, 3rd edition, 1969).

CHAPTER 8

Stocks of Spare Parts

> Now in building of chaises, I tell you what,
> There is always somewhere a weakest spot—
> In hub, tire, felloe, in spring or thill,
> In panel, or crossbar, or floor, or sill,
> In screw, bolt, thoroughbrace—lurking still,
> Find it somewhere you must and will—
> Above or below, or within or without—
> And that's the reason, beyond a doubt
> That a chaise *breaks down*, but doesn't *wear out*.
>
> OLIVER WENDELL HOLMES, *The Deacon's Masterpiece*.

A modern factory resembles a living organism in its need for the continuous replacement of its working parts. Spares flow in as new items and out again as scrap: the flow is intermittent and usually takes place in several stages, hence the need for stocks. For spares, just as for the materials used in manufacture, we must begin to study stocks by looking at this flow as a series of input-output processes which are uncoupled by their stock centres.

These are illustrated in Fig. 41, in which the part in service is classified as a 'stock' held by the plant itself. The output process from this stock is the failure of the part—obviously the 'demand' when it arises can only be for a single part, and the uncertainty of the demand is purely one of time. In theory, we could derive statistical rules about this uncertainty, and indeed a 'theory of replacement' has been developed in which we can apply these rules. It can be very helpful when the failure is of a simple type such as occurs in electric lamp bulbs; in our present state of knowledge, the theory of replacements is not so helpful in other practical situations. There are at least four reasons for this—

(1) The pattern of failure is a complicated one because a single part or assembly may fail for several different reasons. An electric motor, for example, may break down because the windings fail, the brushes wear out, or a connexion breaks.

(2) The 'natural' pattern is disturbed by human intervention. A part which has been in service for a long time may, under a system of planned maintenance, be replaced even though it is still working well.

(3) An automatic 'weeding-out' may occur, as in thermionic valves. They have a relatively high probability of failure during their first few hours of use, after which the survivors settle down to a comparatively long life.

(4) Since failures are rare events, the recorded data are often inadequate.

In spite of these shortcomings, we may find ourselves obliged to set some value on the probability of a failure as a function of time, but we must face the fact that this is often little better than a guess.

We are therefore confronted with the need to provide a control system which will be triggered off by the failure of a part in service and which will cause a replacement to be supplied from stores within some specified minimum time. This is a special type of two-bin system, one in which the ROL is zero, the ROQ is unity, and the rate of consumption is relatively low.

FIG 41 *Replacement of Spares: Processes and Stocks*

Our attention becomes focused on the speed with which our system must respond—how quickly do we need to provide the replacement. To answer this we must begin by asking, "What happens when the part *does* fail?"

If a fuse blows at home, the effect is immediate—the lights go out. Replacement takes five or ten minutes, and during this time we are put to some inconvenience, but not much—the 'cost of breakdown' is low. But if the lights go out suddenly in an operating theatre, the cost may be a human life, and the hospital authorities are justified in installing elaborate and expensive stand-by equipment. These two contrasting cases illustrate a general rule—the quicker a replacement is provided the greater will be the cost of supplying it; the more costly the breakdown, the quicker will the part be needed.

Take as an example the chemical plant shown in the upper half of Fig. 42. The plant makes a profit of £200 an hour and its main component is a reactor fed by two identical pumps. If either pump breaks down, the reactor will stop within a minute or two. It takes eight hours to start the reactor up again, so the minimum cost of failure is £1,600.

A pump with its associated piping and accessories costs £500; one good method of replacement would be to install duplicate pumps which would automatically take over in case of failure. This would cost £1,000, and would be justified as soon as it averted a single reactor failure *which could not have been prevented otherwise.*

Installed spares are not the only answer. The reactor stops almost

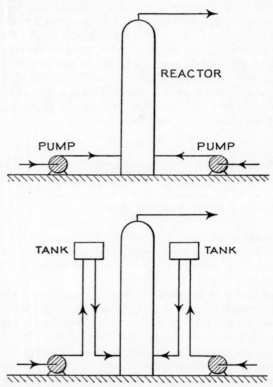

FIG 42 *Effect of Intermediate Feed Tanks on Spare Pumps for a Reactor*

immediately after a pump breaks down, because the two are closely coupled. Can they be uncoupled and if so, how? We know the answer already—by a stock. The lower half of Fig. 42 shows the same plant modified by the addition of two storage tanks; if either pump fails, its part is played by one of the tanks for a limited time— say, half an hour. This will give us time to replace the faulty pump with a spare from the local stores, so only one spare need be carried to serve both pumps. If the combined cost of the tanks comes to less than £500 (the cost of one pump), then it will be less than that of the 'installed spare' system. The availability of one pair of stocks —the materials in the tanks—will have reduced the need for a more expensive stock of spare pumps.

This is an extreme case, in which a breakdown would be so expensive that it could not be permitted in any circumstances. Examples occur in the steel and glass industries as well as in chemical manufacture. In effect, we put an infinitely high cost on breakdowns.

In other cases the failure of a part affects only a small section of the plant immediately, and the effect spreads slowly through the remainder. If a coal-cutting machine breaks down at the coal face, the immediate loss is only the production from that machine; this loss can be isolated, measured and valued because, unlike our chemical plant, the whole mine will not be thrown out of gear. We can consider several possible replacement policies—

(1) Hold a set of spares on every machine—this will give us the most expensive inventory together with the most immediate service and therefore the smallest loss due to breakdowns.

(2) Keep one or more sets at a local (pit-head) stores to serve all the coal-cutters at that colliery. Fewer spares will be needed per machine but service will be slower.

(3) Keep several sets at a central stores which serves a group of consumers; once again, the number of spares per machine will be lower and the delay greater.

(4) Rely entirely on stocks held by the manufacturer or other outside supplier.

Fig. 43 illustrates such a range of possibilities from the installed spare to reliance on the manufacturer. The rational choice of a policy (or maybe a mixture of them) would be dictated by weighing the cost and probability of a breakdown, or the dissatisfaction of a customer as in conventional stock control, against the cost of stocking and supplying the spares for each of the possible lead times. The speed of modern communications has tended to cause a slow drift towards centralization of stocks. For example, the United States Air Force chooses to supply many items to its European bases direct from stores in North America, often within two days of the need arising.

The growth and cheapening of civil air freight facilities is helping to change the methods of giving maintenance service to overseas customers. Air freight is still expensive compared with road, rail and sea, but this does not prevent U.K. car manufacturers from flying a good many consignments of spares every day to customers all over the world.

The actual replacement of a defective part has been shown to be a two-bin system: is there also an analogue of the constant cycle system? This would call for parts to be replaced at regular intervals whether serviceable or not, which is the basis of preventive maintenance. Maintenance systems of this type are still quite rare in

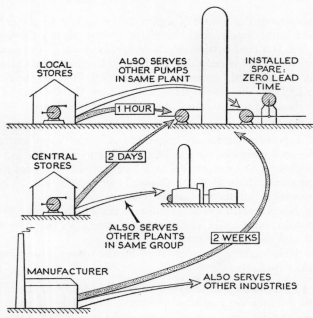

FIG 43 *Multiple Lead Times for Spares*

Britain, but are becoming increasingly popular. They are beyond the scope of this book, but it is worth mentioning in passing that some of the basic ideas of stock control as propounded in the earlier chapters can help when preventive maintenance is being planned.

Let us now turn from the second to the first of the two stock centres shown in Fig. 41, that is, to the stock held in stores. For a manufacturer whose several customers are pursuing policy (4) (page 109), the problem will fall into a conventional pattern; the uncertainties associated with the separate customers will add up to a

frequency distribution similar to those described in Chapter 3. At a
local stores (policy 2) we shall have a one-at-a-time procedure like
that which occurs on the plant itself, and we shall need a stock
control method which deals in ones and twos. This presents its own
special problems, but can be evolved by minimizing the total cost
of breakdown and stockholding as already explained.

Some interesting work along these lines has been done by a group
in France, and a full description is given in the paper by Melèse

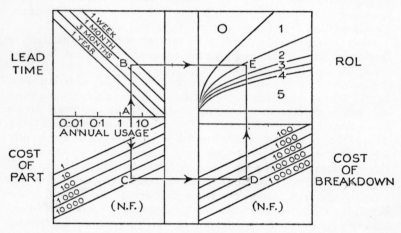

FIG 44 *Graphical Method of Calculating the Re-ordering Level for Spare Parts*

et al.[1] In this paper, the probability of a breakdown was replaced
by the average rate of usage of a spare part. The other factors which
they considered were—

The cost of the part;
its lead time;
the cost of a breakdown; and
the rate of return on capital (10 per cent in this case).

They also assumed that for parts with a low rate of usage the
ROQ would always be one.

The ingenious graph which they produced is shown in Fig. 44; it
reduces what would otherwise be a complicated calculation to a very
simple procedure. We can illustrate this by referring to our example

[1] MELÈSE, J., BARACHE, COMES, ELINA AND HESTAUX, "La Gestion des Stocks
de Pièces," *Proceedings of the Secon International Conference on Operational Research,
Aix-en-Provence*, 1960, p. 309.

of the reactor, assuming that the lead time for a spare pump is three weeks.

We use on the average three pumps a year, so we enter the graph at the point A which corresponds to this and draw a line vertically upwards until it reaches the point B between the diagonal lines: this represents the three weeks' lead time. A line is also drawn downwards until it reaches C, the cost of the part (£500 is about 6,600 new francs) and then horizontally to D, the cost of a breakdown (£1,600 is about 21,000 new francs). Completing the rectangle gives the ROL, point E, which is two. The rule is then, "When the available stock falls to two pumps, order one more."

More recent developments take into account the 'rotation' of assemblies such as pumps which are not always scrapped, but may return to use after repair.

The problem can also be approached in a rather different way. Single failures occurring at regular intervals resemble in some ways the individual customers entering a shop. If the customers arrive faster than the shop assistant can deal with them, a queue will form. This will also happen even when the level of service is apparently adequate, because of the *irregularity* of arrivals. One special case of this is calls arriving at a telephone exchange, although the "queue" occurs only on the operator's indicator board. Queues of this sort were studied by a Danish telephone engineer, A. K. Erlang, at the beginning of this century. His work culminated in a mathematical 'theory of queues', the application of which have gone far beyond Erlang's original field of study.

Breakdowns, then, are 'customers' and spare parts are 'servers'. We can get rid of a queue of customers, or reduce it to a reasonable maximum length, by putting in more servers. If we put in too many servers, they will be idle for long periods—indeed, we can then regard the servers themselves, if we wish, as forming a queue waiting for customers. The theory of queues helps us to find the balance between servers and customers which will keep the total costs as low as possible. To do this, we must find the cost of employing the servers, which is our stockholding cost, and that of dissatisfied customers, which in this case is the cost of a breakdown through lost production, failure to provide an anticipated service, or more general consequences of interrupted operations.

The theory of queues approaches such problems by classifying queues under three main headings: arrival pattern, service pattern and *queue discipline*. The arrival and service patterns correspond respectively to demand and supply; the queue discipline deals with such matters as queue limits and impatient customers, which

need to be interpreted in the light of the spares/breakdown
situation.

Queue Disciplines for Spares

The 'impatient customer' leaves the queue if he is not served within
some specified time. One cannot prevent machines from breaking
down and if they do, they must eventually be serviced, so they join
the queue of waiting customers. 'Impatience' manifests itself as a
need to enter some procedure other than the normal one. In one
case, in a remote part of South America, a resourceful Chief
Engineer faced with a serious breakdown in a mine, went so far
as to have a pattern designed for a vital spare, a mould made, steel
melted in a small cupola furnace, the part cast and then machined
in his own workshops—surely a most unusual case of an 'impatient
customer'! An upper limit on queue length is similar in that it
implies some sort of emergency procedure when the number of
breakdowns demanding a particular spare exceeds some limit.
This can happen when the part needed is common to many
machines, and Cass discusses an interesting case of this, the so-
called 'machine interference' problem in which the spare 'part' is
the attention of a fitter drawn from a limited pool.[1]

The most obvious form of discipline is 'first come, first served',
but there may well be a case for jumping the queue, as when the
last delivery vehicle competes with the managing director's car for
the only sparking-plug left in the stores.

The theory extends beyond the simple case of a single service
channel at which all the 'customers' must present themselves—a
single window in the stores, perhaps—to multi-channel systems and
'closed' queues in which a 'customer' machine after service joins yet
another queue or even rejoins the one it occupied originally.[2]

When the 'customer' is a large modern air liner delayed on the
ground and the 'server' is a spare jet engine costing £250,000 the
virtues of minimizing costs are evident. This has led at least one
international air line to apply the theory of queues on the grand
scale to stocks of 5,000 different spare parts at each of 75 airports.

The policy adopted in this case was to allocate parts to airports,
regardless of cost, so as to hold at some specified low figure the total

[1] Tom Cass, *Statistical Methods for Management* (Cassell, 1969), page 29.

[2] The standard work of reference is Philip M. Morse, *Queues, Inventories and
Maintenance* (Chapman and Hall, 1958); also recommended to the serious student
is A. M. Lee, *Applied Queueing Theory* (Macmillan, 1966), which treats the subject
mathematically but in a highly readable fashion.

number of occasions in a year that a part was not available when needed. This means that the cost of delay was estimated *implicitly*, just as the cost of running out of stock was implied when we chose a risk level from Fig. 14. Parts requirements were calculated from a formula derived from the theory of queues, which related—

The probability of a shortage (at each demand);

The number of demands per week;

The average replenishment time in weeks; and

The number of spare parts to be held.

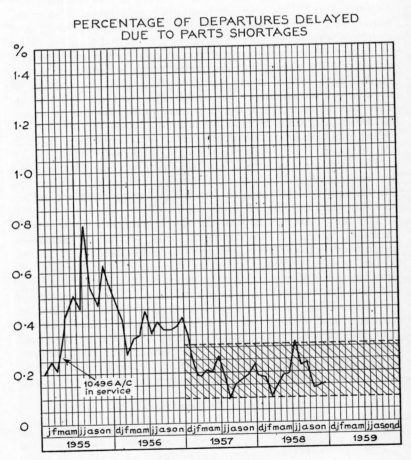

PERCENTAGE OF DEPARTURES DELAYED
DUE TO PARTS SHORTAGES

FIG 45 *Airline Efficiency Improved by Good Stock Control*

The number of demands per week was forecast from the number of landings of each type of aircraft at each airport, suitably adjusted for local conditions. Fig. 45 shows the results: these are particularly striking because the improvement from 1957 onwards was obtained with no increase in the total inventory.

The NCB System

The National Coal Board in Britain has been a pioneer in devising and applying practical systems for dealing systematically with the supply of spares. In doing so, they have drawn on the whole range of stock control theory. Members of the Board's Field Investigation Unit have applied the most sophisticated mathematics to their data, but have always been at pains to study the real nature of the problems by finding out, in great detail, what actually happens when a machine breaks down underground. The scrupulous care of their enquiries has enabled them to assign costs to breakdowns, using loss of production as a basis and thus arriving at an optimum risk level.

The resultant system relies on an important, yet simple two-way classification. A spare is a *priority* item if in normal working circumstances its breakdown would halt a production face until repairs were effected; *non-priority* items are those in which imminent failure can be detected in time to permit of repair during a non-production shift, or whose repair may be delayed until the end of a working shift without loss of production, or which are not repaired at the face itself. (Incidentally, the Unit's enthusiasm for systematic control has even led it to apply similar theories to the provision of 'spare' coal-faces!)

The speed with which a replacement can be brought up is obviously important and contributes to a classification into *portable* items which can be carried to the face by hand and *non-portable* ones which need a 'tub'.

Three levels of source are considered, as in Fig. 42: the colliery itself, a central stores and the manufacturer of the item. Consequently, the lead time of the latter is also included as a factor in the 'broad' classification of spares.

The system is basically two-bin, with an advanced ROL (*see* page 78) and working in conjunction with a regular delivery system which constitutes a supplementary constant-cycle system for some of the spares. It has been reduced to a few simple tables which are separated according to the broad classification just described, i.e. priority—portability—lead time—type of store (colliery or central). One selects the appropriate table, enters it with the annual usage of the item and its price, then reads off ROL and ROQ. The policy figure for capital at 10 per cent per annum, is embodied in the calculations, as it was in the Melèse chart (Fig. 44) and is therefore not needed by the user of the tables.

Specimen extracts from the working tables appear in Tables XIV and XV, so as to give an idea of the magnitudes of ROL and ROQ in relation to price and usage. They are not, however, suitable for general use, being heavily summarized, specially calculated for the Coal Board's own peculiar circumstances, and probably out of date anyway.

The system was installed in stages. The first pilot trials were on a small scale; while confirming the general soundness of the method, the trials also showed what it needed in the way of minor modifications. Although the stock control of spare parts may raise its own special questions which are answered by specialized methods, such methods do not depart in any way from the general principles which we laid down in the opening chapters.

TABLE XIV: *Stock levels at collieries (for portable spares)*

Price	Annual Demand					
	Non-priority Items			Priority Items		
	10	50	200	10	50	200
10p	*1,1*	*3,8*	*9,20*	*3,1*	*6,6*	*13,20*
£1	*0,1*	*3,3*	*8,6*	*2,1*	*5,3*	*12,6*
£10	*0,1*	*2,1*	*6,2*	*1,1*	*4,1*	*10,3*
£50	O.A.R.	*0,1*	*4,2*	*1,1*	*4,1*	*10,1*

TABLE XV: *Stock levels at central stores (priority portable and all non-priority items)*

Price	Annual Demand					
	Lead Time 1 month			Lead Time 2 months		
	10	50	200	10	50	200
10p	*3,30*	*10,50*	*40,130*	*5,30*	*20,50*	*80,150*
£1	*3,10*	*8,20*	*35,45*	*4,10*	*15,25*	*70,50*
£10	*2,4*	*6,8*	*30,20*	*2,5*	*12,10*	*60,20*
£50	*0,2*	*5,5*	*25,15*	*1,3*	*8,6*	*45,15*
£500	*0,1*	*3,4*	*15,15*	*1,1*	*8,4*	*30,15*

Notes (*a*) The number in italics before the comma is the ROL (*b*) The number after the comma is the ROQ 'O.A.R.' means "order as required".

This summary table, reproduced by permission of the National Coal Board, is not necessarily suitable for general use (*see* text).

CHAPTER 9

Size of Storage Space

> My people ask counsel at their stocks, and
> their staff declareth unto them:
> HOSEA, iv, 12.

In this chapter, the calculation of required storage space is discussed in terms of one practical example, to wit, tanks for
petroleum products or other liquid manufactures. Two reasons lie
behind this choice. The first is that much of my more recent personal
experience has lain in this area and the second is that the method
described here has been adopted by the three major British oil
companies. Consequently, it has been thoroughly tested both by
computer simulations and subsequent practical experience which
has amply confirmed its dependability. The principles are not
exclusive to oil, but are universal; the only possible snag in their
wider application is that it is easier to let several solid products
share the same floor space than to use a single storage tank for
different hydrocarbons. This difficulty is not insuperable and the
graphical methods described here can be applied as widely as those
given in earlier chapters.

Case example

Batches of product are delivered from the factory to a storage tank,
from which orders for customers are filled. The batch size is 100
tons, the variation in this being negligible. The Production Planning
Office decides when to call for the manufacture of a batch, and it
will usually be delivered to stock a week later. This lead time varies
considerably, being normally distributed about the mean with a
standard deviation of 0·25 week.

An analysis of deliveries to customers in the past shows that the
offtake has a slight upward trend but no perceptible seasonal effect;
it has remained fairly steady at 330 tons a week, with random
fluctuations equivalent to a standard deviation of 71 tons per
week.

We build up the required storage space from four components
(*see* Fig. 46)—

118

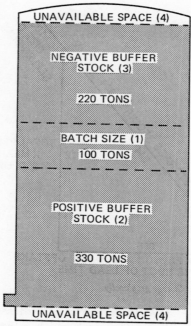

Fig 46 *Components of Storage*

(1) The space needed to accommodate a batch when it arrives, in this case 100 tons.

(2) The *positive buffer stock*, providing a reserve against high offtake, late arrival of a batch, or both.

(3) The *negative buffer stock*, being a reserve of storage space against low offtake and early arrival, or both.

(4) An allowance for 'bottoms', heating coils, 'ullage' and other unavailable storage space. This is a matter of engineering design and special properties of the product to be stored; it will be ignored here.

We are fortunate in this case because a statistician has already condensed the figures for us into means and standard deviations, but unlucky in that the buffer stocks have to cover us simultaneously for variations in both sales (or 'offtake') and lead time.

As managers, we are obliged to set a risk factor or *policy factor* and, as in the simpler case of chocolic acid, this is a multiplier of a standard deviation. We are concerned here with the *standard*

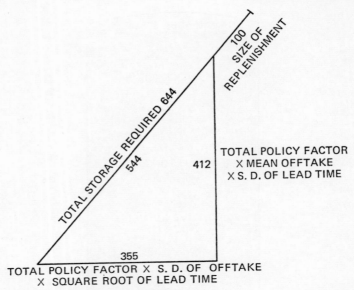

FIG 47 *Finding required Storage graphically*

deviation of demand in the lead time, but we can still say roughly that a policy factor of 2 will give us a stock which is inadequate once in every 40 replenishment periods, whereas for a factor of 3 the risk is once in every 740 periods. In the case under discussion 740 periods is about 14 years, so a policy factor of 3 may be said to represent virtual certainty.

It is convenient to calculate the sum of the two buffer stocks by adding the separate policy factors. Let us suppose that in this example we have taken 3 for the positive and 2 for the negative buffer stocks, a total of 5.

(1) Calculate—
Total Policy Factor × Standard Deviation of Offtake × Square Root of Lead Time = 5 × 71 × 1 = 335

(2) Calculate—
Total Policy Factor × Mean Offtake × Standard Deviation of Lead Time = 5 × 330 × 0·25 = 412

(3) Draw lines proportional in length to these two figures, at right angles to each other. Complete the right-angled triangle and measure the hypotenuse. (544). See Fig. 47.

(4) Add the batch size to obtain the total storage needed (644 tons). In round figures, the total storage needed is 650 tons, and this should suffice during normal running.

You will no doubt have noticed that the first step gives the total buffer stocks (positive plus negative) which would be needed if the lead time were constant and only the offtake (sales) varied randomly. The second step, on the other hand, gives the total buffer stocks for a fixed offtake and a variable lead time. Step (3) is the graphical equivalent of adding the squares of these and taking the square root of their sum, an operation which might just as well have been done arithmetically, except that our triangle has its uses, as we shall see when visualizing what happens when the figures (which we call the *parameters*) relating to the problem are changed.

On the same principle we can extend Fig. 47 to show the cost, in terms of storage, of a delay. If we believe that the expected lead time is liable to be extended for a week in abnormal circumstances, we might well consider enlarging our storage capacity correspondingly.

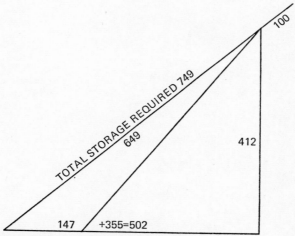

FIG 48 *Sensitivity to Change in Lead Time*

(1) Calculate—

With a lead time of 2 weeks ($5 \times 71 \times 1{\cdot}414 = 502$) and use this to draw a new triangle as in Fig. 48. The buffer stock now becomes 650 tons and the total storage 750 tons.

The shape of our triangle will also give us a rough indication of the effects of changing certain factors. A tall thin triangle means that the buffer stocks will be sensitive to the variables contributing to the longer side and insensitive to those in the shorter side.

5*

We call this *sensitivity testing* because we find out how *sensitive* our calculated storage requirement is to unreliable estimates of the parameters. In Fig. 47, the vertical side is the longer and it is affected by changes in the *average* offtake (though not its variation) and the fluctuations undergone by the lead time. The shorter horizontal side is affected by the average magnitude of the lead time and the fluctuation of offtake. The policy factor in this elementary example is common to both although this is not necessarily so in every case.

The theory on which this method is based has been presented by Fetter and Dalleck in a way which is mathematically adequate without being obscure.[1]

[1] R. B. FETTER and W. C. DALLECK, *Decision Models for Inventory Management* (Irwin, 1961), p. 105.

CHAPTER 10

Stock Control and Management

It takes a man of vision
To make a decision.

OGDEN NASH, *Good Intentions.*

There are three people in an average small or medium-sized company whose actions and mental attitudes can have a big effect on the general level of stocks.

First, the Sales Manager. His job, he will tell you, is to make sure that every customer gets the goods he wants in the right quantity, of the right quality and at the right time; he may also add, "at the right price." The Sales Manager will try to make sure that goods are always available in stock to meet any demand, however unexpected, and to this end he will exert pressure on the Production Department. We saw in Chapter 3 that perfect service to the customer is an impossible ideal, so the salesman's pressure will always be tending to drive stock levels upwards.

Second, the Production Manager. For many years, production engineers have extolled the virtues of long manufacturing runs, culminating in their supreme achievement, the continuous assembly line of the mass-production factory. Yet for most of us, mass production is out of the question—we have to use the same plant to make a variety of products. When the plant needs to be changed over from one product to another, it will have to hold 'carry-over' or 'cycle' stocks (see Appendix 4) and the total amount of such stocks is directly proportional to the length of the production run. Thus in striving for the shop-floor efficiency associated with long manufacturing runs, the Production Manager will always be tending to drive stock levels upwards.

Third, the Buyer. His reasons for wanting to order in large amounts are obvious—the man with a big order to place is in a strong position when it comes to negotiating terms advantageous for his firm. In doing so, he may well be forcing the Sales Manager of his supplier to press for larger stocks, but his efforts will also be felt nearer home. Fig. 6 (page 20) shows the average stock (ignoring buffer stock) to be half the size of the order. So in trying to buy advantageously the Buyer will always be tending to drive stock levels upwards.

The last nine words of all these three paragraphs are the same. The men responsible for selling, producing and buying all have direct control of stock levels and each of them, in trying to achieve efficiency within his own department, may cause stocks to go up.

That is not to say that these three executives will necessarily behave shortsightedly and clutter up their departments with excessive stocks. Nevertheless, each has an *incentive* to do so, and there is evidence that lazy or irresponsible managers do exist. For instance, one American research worker, looking for practical examples of job-shop scheduling problems, reported that in many cases the manager had so thoroughly buffered his plant with stocks that the need for tight scheduling had disappeared, making life easier for the manager at the company's expense.

Within the same firm there will be someone—it may be the Secretary, the Managing Director or the entire Board—whose job is to control his company's finances. Let us call him the Finance Director: we see him in Fig. 49, in a position senior to the other three

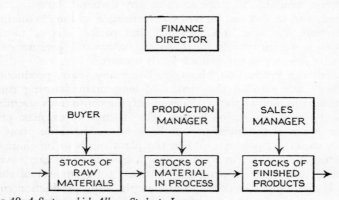

Fig 49 *A System which Allows Stocks to Increase*

executives. Because of his high status, he can exert no *direct* control over stock levels, yet it is from him that we must expect any pressure to reduce investment in inventory. Since the Finance Director cannot affect stocks directly, he must work by influencing the three managers; this calls for a line of communication and control to them, *specifically devoted to inventory policy*.

When the inventory is costly and complicated, the extra load which this duty imposes on the Finance Director may be too great for him to handle efficiently without neglecting his other functions. He will then need a subordinate who can translate his general decisions on policy into detailed instructions. The subordinate would be the Materials Controller: this title is better than the more usual 'Stock Controller' because, as we have seen, he controls the *flow* of materials rather than the stocks themselves. The new organization is shown in Fig. 50.

The final outflow (sales) of goods cannot be controlled by the manufacturer to any great extent, so the emphasis will usually fall on the input, that is to say, on buying. In a small company where the managers are few and versatile, the overall control of materials may become vested in the Buyer for this reason.

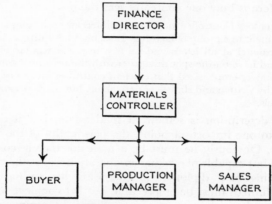

Fig 50 *A System for Keeping Stocks under Control*

This analysis of the fundamental managerial problem is still valid and has therefore been brought forward virtually unchanged from the first edition of this book, but within the last decade there have been important developments, not so much in the nature of the problem itself as in the steps taken to meet it. All the professional associations concerned—the various Engineering Institutions, the Institute of Marketing and the Institute of Purchasing and Supply have become aware of the financial strictures on stock and all have taken steps to ensure a balance between capital investment and the purely departmental advantages described above.

It is the Buyers who have taken the lead, not least by beginning with a reorganization of themselves and a widening of their field of view. The old Purchasing Officers Association merged with the

Institute of Public Supplies in 1967 to form the new Institute of Purchasing and Supply, discussed later under 'Professional Bodies' (*see* page 146). Insofar as the offices of Buyer and Materials Controller in Fig. 50 are combined—the desirability of doing this has been hotly argued and some of the dust of battle still lingers—the authority over the other executives implied by Fig. 50 extends only to the supply function. For other restricted functions the dominant executive might well be one of the other two; thus, the Sales or Marketing Manager might have the last word in matters relating to quality or distribution.

Whatever title the Materials Controller may hold—Chief Purchasing Officer, Inventory Controller, perhaps even Stock and Production Controller—his rights and duties should be clearly defined. Here is how one company sees them—

> An Inventory Controller must be appointed for each company, factory or department in a group of factories. He should have direct contact with other personnel at all levels and be free to make regular tours of the factory and have on-the-spot discussion with the personnel concerned. It cannot be over-emphasized that efficient control of inventory cannot be obtained by written and statistical data alone, but needs personal contact at all levels.

Such a description is somewhat inadequate, but it does draw attention to one important point, the personality of the Materials Controller. Obviously he must be a man not merely co-operative in himself, but capable of evoking co-operation from others; he must be something of a diplomat in exercising his authority which, although limited, must be enforceable if it is to achieve any results at all. Since the management of inventory is becoming recognized more and more as a team effort, the status of the Materials Controller will often be that of a 'first among equals'. If he combines materials control (or, if you prefer, the 'supply function') with that of heading a specialist department, he must have the breadth of vision to subordinate purely departmental advantage to the interests of the firm in general, and therefore the strength of character to resist the pressures which his own colleagues may exert upon him.

The theory of organizations is now tending to emphasize the picture of a business as a set of functional roles connected by lines of communication. Fig. 51 shows the Materials Controller as he would be seen in the light of this new theory, in his role as the controller of stock levels. The first thing to note about this diagram is that it distinguishes between internal communications and those to the outside world. The Materials Controller in his role as Buyer

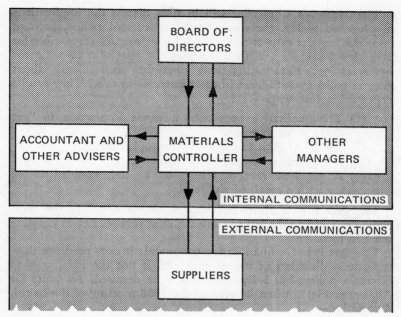

FIG 51 *Sources of External Finance*

will naturally be more authoritative in his dealings with suppliers than with his peers within the company, since he speaks to the former on behalf of the business as a whole, but internally as the guardian of only one (or a few) of its functions.

For the sake of simplicity, I have omitted from Fig. 51 the Materials Controller's own subordinates, such as his office and stores staff. This allows the lines of communication to be shown, without too much controversy, as two-way links.

Such a view accords with today's idea of management as an exercise in co-operation rather than the pure application of authority described by the centurion in Matthew *viii*, 9. The Controller will not only pass on the policy dictates of the Board; he will help to formulate them by offering technical advice and reporting back on their effectiveness, efficiency and snags. In doing so he will, as we have already seen, need to collaborate with the company's accountant, but other advisers may need to be consulted also. Although the diagram implies that they will be within the company, outside experts such as consultants may be subsumed under this heading.

The Materials Controller will in turn discuss the implications of proposed policy, the consequences of current policy, perhaps even the legacies of past policy with his colleagues responsible for other functions. He will therefore play the part of a co-ordinator by receiving, transmitting and discussing instructions about general policy: what form will these instructions take? They can be expressed in four ways—

(1) The qualitative approach: a vague instruction to "get stocks down a bit somehow".

(2) An upper limit to the total value of inventory.

(3) A required average rate of turnover.

(4) A required rate of return on capital, coupled where necessary with a specified risk level.

The first two of these policies are almost certainly the most common, whereas the last two are the most precise. Let us examine them in turn.

The first is not a quantitative command: it does no more than indicate a direction of movement. This is not the ideal way to dictate a policy, but is by no means to be despised. To quote Sir Alexander Fleck, when he opened the 1958 meeting of the British Association—

. . . even the first qualitative steps of the scientific approach can often lead directly to improvements in business efficiency.

Much can be achieved by qualitative methods—merely educating middle management staff in the high cost of stocks can cause second thoughts about the size of orders or production runs. The following extract is taken from a report on the stock control methods of a warehousing and distributing company—

The recent introduction of a fairly substantial interest charge or credit on stocks above or below Budget has had a very marked effect in making Managers stock conscious and in resisting some of the Central Buying Department's suggestions about taking in additional stocks to obtain price advantages. There is also evidence that the interest charge is getting prompter action where actual sales prove to be lower than the purchasing commitments. In the past, Branches have tended to continue to accept the consignments against original forward estimates even although the incoming quantities are above offtake, without doing very much about it, taking the attitude that these transactions were arranged by the Buying Department and that there was very little that could be done to change matters, and that in any case the stocks would be cleared out eventually. Now they are pushing the Buying Department to cut back on orders or to move the goods elsewhere.

You may well argue with considerable justification that this is policy (4) rather than (1), which shows how hard (and how unnecessary at times) it is to draw these arbitrary divisions. But ask yourself which probably did more to reduce stocks—the actual level at which the interest rate was set or the impact of its introduction?

The second command is no more than a modification of the first, since the upper limit usually turns out to be the present value of the inventory. In the absence of a well-defined control policy, the inventory has almost certainly become grossly inflated before jolting the Finance Director into action. Still, such a command does give the Materials Controller a definite starting point from which to progress to a more scientific policy. At least the line of communication is open.

Few, if any modern businessmen would accept a literal interpretation of Oliver Cromwell's dictum that "a few honest men are better than numbers"; the earlier chapters of this book have shown how aspects of a business previously left to 'feel' are reducible to numbers, and many managers would feel a greater affinity with Tennyson's "All in quantity, careful of my motion, Like the skater on ice that hardly bears him." But what shall these numbers and quantities be? One popular criterion is the ratio Total Value of Sales (usually in a year) to Total Value of Inventory, that is, the number of times the stock is 'turned over' in a year. This figure is called the 'stock turnover' or 'rate of turnover' or simply 'turnover': this abbreviation is unfortunate because it is also used widely to describe the volume of sales. Neither is the ratio itself a very good indicator, although it does have the merit of ensuring, if it is enforced, that stocks expand to allow for increased manufacturing activity and that they contract when demand falls. Even so, the best (or *optimum*) level of stocks is more likely to vary, not directly as the sales, but roughly in proportion to their square root. In spite of these drawbacks, the stock turnover does hold some value as a rule-of-thumb for setting policy and comparing company performances: I have analysed many sets of accounts over the last twenty years and have been surprised to find how often the stock turnover ratio lies between about 4 and 5 for large manufacturing enterprises such as I.C.I., Bowaters and Metal Box. It would, however, be unwise to take this as in any way a universal standard: one Scottish firm of wholesalers of food products has set its overall average stock at three weeks, a stock turnover ratio of 17! By contrast, a big group of machine-tool manufacturers, trading at the level of tens of millions of pounds a year, once had a stock turnover ratio of about one (and, it may be added, a steadily falling trend in the value of its shares.)

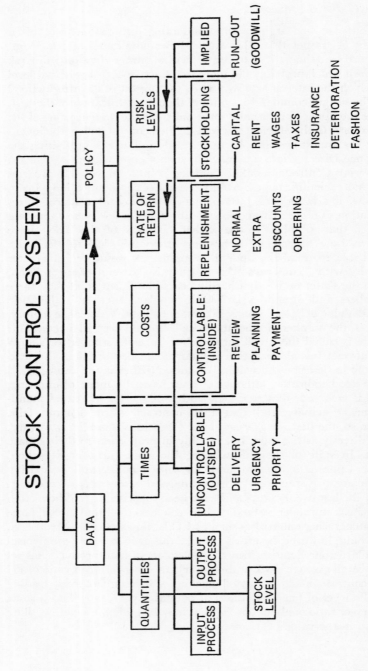

Fig 52 *Managerial Information required for a Stock Control System*

The Overall Optimum

Attempts to reduce inventory policy to a single 'optimum' figure
have not been outstandingly successful, and you need only refer to
Fig. 52 to see why. This diagram summarizes all the information
needed by the Materials Controller: in order to 'optimize' his
control system he will have to—

(1) Reduce every item to a monetary value—even that for
'goodwill' which appears on the extreme right as an implied cost
of 'run-out' (i.e. no stock.)

(2) Combine all the items into a single 'control function' by
performing suitable mathematical operations on them as discussed in the next paragraph.

The Control Function

The easiest way to combine several related figures is to add them up,
but a quick glance at those in Fig. 52 will show that they are not all
of equal importance, so they may have to be *weighted*, and the
weights are bound to contain a large element of managerial judgment. But this is not all: we have seen already that measures of
variation are as important as averages, sometimes more so, and now
we must add to this a brief mention of the three sorts of control used
in systems analysis. They are—

(1) Proportional control.
(2) Rate control.
(3) Integral control.

Proportional control is the simplest: a big stock is twice as demanding as a similar one half its size.

Rate control means that the stock needed to back *rising* sales must
be greater than that for *static* sales at the same level (or lower if
they are felling)—so the manager may need to know about
differential coefficients, which express rates of change numerically.

Integral control puts into mathematical terms such simple truths
as 'being out of stock for one day is not as bad as being out of stock
for three days' and although its symbols may look rather frightening
to the non-mathematician, that is still no excuse for divorcing them
from common sense.

Control theory appears in full war-paint as cybernetics, systems
analysis or the latest crop of confusing initials, but the executive
who has to apply the control has every right to press his technical
adviser for an explanation of his symbols in plain English limited, if
necessary, to words of one syllable.

It may be some consolation to the non-mathematical manager to

know that when faced by the possible complications I have just
outlined, many management scientists have felt just as reluctant as
he to tackle the problem of the overall optimum. That is no excuse
for giving up the pursuit of this ideal but in the meantime, the last
of my four options has much to recommend it as a practical policy.

Rate of Return on Capital

The last method, the rate of return on capital, has the great advantage that it assesses inventory on the same basis as the other physical
assets of the firm. Chapter 2 showed that a specified rate of return
was needed in order to calculate economic lot sizes, and Table III
(page 25) showed its effect upon stockholding costs. Opinions are
divided about how the return should be decided: should it reflect
the current cost of borrowing and be in the range 5 to 10 per cent?
Or should it be assessed like new machinery and be required to show
a return of 15 to 30 per cent? The difference is important: the
second viewpoint will cause the total value of inventory to be
roughly half as compared with the first. Both types of policy are in
current use and the subject can always be relied on to sustain a lively
argument whenever experts on stock control forgather.

'Return on capital' has been used in this book as a concise
description of the cost of holding stocks, for two principal reasons—
it is often the predominant cost and the most readily variable. This
should not obscure the fact that it is only one component of a whole
group of costs (and not always the main one when we have goods
which combine large bulk with low value).

Physical Costs

The other component constitutes the so-called 'physical' costs of
holding materials in stock and contains such items as the following—

> Provision of storage space.
> Provision of storage racks and bins.
> Wages of storekeepers and helpers.
> Cost of handling facilities within the stores.
> Cost of stock records, stationery and files, etc.
> Wages of record clerks.
> Rent, rates, and taxes on the storage space.
> Insurance of stocks.
> Cost of deterioration of materials in stores.
> Cost of writing down in value because of obsolescence.
> Cost of keeping the stock in good condition.
> Loss of interest on money tied up in excess stock.

Some of these elements may be wholly or partly independent of stock levels: the 'existence costs' of a warehouse (e.g. rent, wages) often fall into the former category and it may be more realistic to apportion them to the 'cost of an order' or some similar fixed item.

Insofar as physical handling cost varies with stock levels, its total may be added to the cost of capital in order to arrive at an overall stockholding cost. However, it is my experience that this component rarely exceeds about 2 per cent of the stock value per annum and is more likely to lie in the range 1–1½ per cent. Thus its effect on stock levels is usually trivial, as the following example will show.

With 8 per cent as the rate of return on capital, suppose the physical costs to be 2 per cent: thus the total stockholding cost is 10 per cent (per annum, of course.)

Now if by improving stores efficiency we can halve the physical costs, the total stockholding cost will fall to 9 per cent per annum. The value of the inventory will rise because the advantage it confers can now be got more cheaply and since $\sqrt{10}$ is 3·16 and $\sqrt{9}$ is 3·00, the increase will be 0·16 ÷ 3, which is about one-twentieth of the current value. This apparent paradox (increased efficiency leading to increased inventory) may be resolved by a change in financial policy. With the cost of capital raised to 9 per cent, inventory will be held at its present value and this stiffer financial policy will have repercussions (hopefully, beneficial ones) in other parts or operations of the company.

Thus we can see how even the details of running the stores may impinge on financial policy, which makes it appropriate at this stage to discuss the principles to which chartered accountants adhere in dealing with the valuation of stocks.

Accounting Principles

The Council of The Institute of Chartered Accountants in England and Wales[1] publishes a set of *Recommendations on Accounting Principles*, of which section N22 deals with stock-in-trade and work in progress. The notes are prepared by the Institute primarily for the guidance of its members in presenting a 'true and fair view' (words which are repeated and emphasized) of a business to its stockholders. Nevertheless, they are presented with such admirable lucidity and freedom from technical jargon, that I strongly recommend any manager who really wants to feel in control of his inventory to study them in the original. What follows is a summary in my own words with a few managerial comments added; the Institute has graciously given me permission to quote directly in places, such

[1] City House, 56/66 Goswell Road, London, E.C.1., England.

verbatim extracts being indented to distinguish them from the main body of the text, and beginning with a statement of the Institute's general approach—

In the financial accounts of industrial and commercial undertakings few matters require more careful consideration than the amount to be attributed to stock-in-trade and work in progress. Circumstances vary so widely that no one basis of arriving at the amount is suitable for all types of business nor even for all undertakings within a particular trade or industry. Unless the basis adopted is appropriate to the circumstances of the particular undertaking and used consistently from period to period, the accounts will not give a true and fair view either of the state of affairs of the undertaking as on the balance sheet date or of the trend of its trading results from period to period. The need to give a true and fair view is the overriding consideration applicable in all circumstances.

In order to arrive at the amount to be carried forward, as on the balance sheet date, for stock-in-trade and work in progress it is necessary to ascertain (from stock-taking at the end of the period or from stock records maintained and verified during the period) the quantities on hand and to make a proper calculation of the amount. It cannot be emphasized too strongly that all stocks belonging to the business should be taken into account, whatever their location or nature. This Recommendation does not deal with the methods of ascertaining the quantities on hand but is confined to an examination of the factors to be considered when computing the amount. The word 'stock' is used hereafter to embrace stock-in-trade and work in progress.

NORMAL BASIS

The basis normally used for the determination of the amount to be carried forward for stock is its cost less any part thereof which properly needs to be written off at the balance sheet date. It is in computing cost and the amount, if any, to be written off that practical difficulties arise.

The initial cost is made up of materials, whether they be for resale or use in manufacture, plus expenditure directly incurred in acquiring them and that bane of accountants and managers alike, 'overheads'. There are four main headings under which the latter are subsumed: production, administration, selling and finance charges. The first covers such indirect expenses as rent, rates, depreciation, insurance and supervision and the second recognizes that not all the costs associated with acquiring materials can be allocated to them item by item. The controversial topic of finance charges has already been touched upon briefly; as for selling expenses, they are almost bound to depend on whether or not a 'marginal view' is taken.

The Marginal View

It is easy to say when considering storage as an item of production expenses, "Oh, well, we have some free space in the warehouse anyway: it won't cost us any more to put something into it." This is a 'marginal' view, recognized in accounting by saying that as long as unused storage space exists, the *marginal cost* of occupying it is zero. Likewise, a firm with external facilities for selling and distribution may regard the *marginal* cost of adding another product to the range being handled as zero. In overseas markets this attitude can lead to what is benevolently referred to as 'marginal selling', or less kindly as 'dumping'. There are obvious dangers attached to the marginal view; the first is that if it is carried on to saturation point, the marginal cost faces an unreasonably high stepwise increase, as when a warehouse is suddenly found to be full; the second is that it is often logically possible to regard the marginal cost of any existing facility extended to any individual product as being zero.

The Proportional View

In stock control, all indirect costs which are related to stock but *not* viewed as marginal are candidates for inclusion in the cost of an order. The alternative to the marginal view is the *proportional* view, under which some costs are seen as applying to a group of materials (even the whole range of inventory perhaps) and apportioned to individuals by some consistent rule. This really is difficult to do, for no matter how detached, objective, cool or scientific the manager may make his standpoint, words like 'suitable', 'normal' and 'appropriate' will persist in creeping in and forcing him to recognize the individuality and diversity of the businesses in which stocks are held. This being so, I can do no more than urge collaboration in the highest degree between the manager and his accountant, and this is a topic to be discussed in more detail later.

A key word in the Institute's Recommendations about overheads is 'recoverable': in management, the word 'avoidable' is closely allied to it, so one asks not only "If we spend this now shall we get it back later?" but also "Is this expenditure on stock an essential part of the total managerial action (e.g. distribution, insurance against breakdown or failure of supply) being contemplated?" Again, the notion of a stock as a means of 'buying time' will intrude, with its attendant difficulty of putting a value on time in the affairs being administered.

This is perhaps an appropriate point at which to repeat the distinction between *financial* accounts, which present a picture of a company to those who have a stake in it and to the outside world in general, and the *internal* accounts (sometimes called *cost* accounts) which any manager needs if he is to do his job properly. 'Financial' is an etymological relation of 'final' because it has to do with the settlement of a debt, and any businessman who tries to cheat his creditors by manipulating stock values will only end by cheating himself. It is undesirable as well as unnecessary for stocks to be taken 'at the directors' valuation', since such a method may well attract suspicion. Five accepted methods are available: unit cost, FIFO, average cost, standard cost and adjusted selling price. A 'unit' cost is built up by aggregating the individual costs of each 'article, batch, parcel or other unit' that goes to make up the stock item being valued. A 'standard' cost resembles it in being an aggregation of individual components, where the latter word may include elements of processing as well as of materials, but in standard costing the values are predetermined or budgeted figures and ought to be revised regularly.

FIFO stands for 'first in, first out' and depends on the assumption that whatever is withdrawn from stock for use or sale has been in longest. An alternative, LIFO or 'last in, first out' has obviously undesirable features. It is mentioned here and in the Recommendations as a system in use in some overseas countries, but the conclusion drawn is that LIFO tends to undervalue stock. It has a close relation in NIFO, which means 'next in, first out'.

Average cost applies within an accounting period, the 'average' being that of the stock brought forward at the beginning of the period and that acquired within the period; so if you bought chocolic acid for the first time in 1971 at 24 new pence a ton, entered 1972 with 100 tons in stock and bought another 100 tons in that year at 36p a ton, the average value ascribed to any subsequent withdrawal from stock in 1971 would be 30p a ton, whereas the FIFO value would be 24p.

The fifth method, *adjusted selling price*, is widely used in retail businesses, and derives a sort of 'cost' by deducting the normal margin of gross profit from the best estimate of the stock's current selling price.

The valuer also has the option of reducing the stock to its *net realizable value*, especially useful when some proportion of the initial outlay is irrecoverable. To do so without expert advice is risky. Unpleasant though it may be to have to acknowledge uneconomic buying or production, its occurrence must be recognized at times, and this most important matter is again worth a direct quotation from the Accounting Principles—

Skill in buying or efficiency in production are most important matters in many businesses; the inclusion of stock in the accounts on a replacement price basis (where lower than net realizable value and cost) may be considered to reflect inefficiency in these respects on the ground that it involves the writing down of stock by an amount which represents approximately the result of misjudged buying or inefficient production.

The Recommendations go on to discuss special bases used in some businesses such as tea, rubber and mining, those in which by-products are a problem because they may affect the valuation of the main product, and businesses in which long-term contracts play an important part. They also mention 'base stock': this can be defined as 'the amount you have to fill something with so that it will work' like, for example, the circulating water in a central heating system or the chemicals in a continuous reactor. The word 'it' in this context may stand for a whole plant as well as a single item of equipment, and 'stocks' of such an essential type as this, not being uncouplers, and outside the scope of this book: the only control which can be exercised on base stocks lies in the initial decision to instal the system which contains them or its subsequent entire removal.

Co-operation with the Accountant

No summary can do justice to the painstaking detail and scrupulous honesty of the Institute's notes, but they do necessarily tend to show a bias towards what might be called the 'external' view of the organization which holds the stocks. The stock valuation must not only give a 'true and fair view' but must be seen to do so, whereas the controller concerned with a firm's internal workings may feel the latter to be of minor importance.

Whether the manager agrees or not, and whether the accountant considers his role as primarily that of a 'financial accountant' or a 'cost accountant', co-operation between the two is not merely desirable, it is unavoidable if they are to do their jobs properly. The manager needs the right figures, and the accountant is the expert at producing them: he will often come up with surprisingly useful advice about estimating the actual *amount* of a stock as well as its value (for instance, by pointing out that the only occasions on which a completely error-free estimate can be made is when the stock level is zero). There also may well be taxation aspects on which his advice may cause money to be saved.

Another practical way in which he can help is in gathering and transmitting data. Inventory management needs a 'management information system' but this is just a new label for something which has been a fact of life to accountants for generations. Setting up and maintaining an information system for stock (and production) control will often be taken in his stride by the accountant once the manager has made his requirements clear.

Although the comments above refer exclusively to Section N22, entitled "Treatment of stock-in-trade and work in progress in financial accounts",[1] a glance at other entries in the index to the Recommendations will disclose how widely useful the Accountants' advice may be, covering as it does such matters as Depreciation, Obsolescence, Changes in the Purchasing Power of Money and the special problems of stock valuation in tea, rubber and mining companies. Before leaving the Recommendations, let us conclude with these final words of wisdom in direct quotation—

> A true and fair view also implies the consistent application of generally-accepted principles. Assets are normally shown at cost less amounts charged against revenue to amortize expenditure over the effective lives of the assets or to provide for diminution in their value. A balance sheet is therefore mainly an historical document which does not purport to show the realizable value of assets such as goodwill, land, buildings, plant and machinery; nor does it normally purport to show the realizable value of assets such as stock-in-trade. Thus a balance sheet is not a statement of the net worth of the undertaking and this is normally so even where there has been a revaluation of assets and the balance sheet amount are based on the revaluation instead of on cost.[2] (Section N18, paragraph 4).

Presumptious though it may be to summarize such an exhaustive treatment in a single phrase, an eight-word rule of thumb is: "Cost or market value, whichever is the lower."

What of the people who are to put these policies to work? The ability of the Materials Control staff will depend upon the level at which they are operating. The Controller himself should be a man of high calibre—one has only to consider the inventory as the costly machine described in Chapter 1 to appreciate the level of intelligence needed to keep it under proper control. At present, the title 'Stock Controller' or 'Production Controller' all too frequently describes a conscientious and overworked man tackling a job which is far beyond him. He has probably been pitchforked into it without proper training, because the need for such training has never been appreciated and few courses are available. With this background, it

---

[1] Issued 16th November, 1960.

[2] Issued October, 1958.

is only to be expected that the work sometimes turns out badly—what *is* surprising is that the unfortunate Stock Controller manages to do it at all. His own common sense and intimate knowledge of his factory help him to avert disaster, but leave him little time to reflect on the causes which almost led to it.

The Use of Consultants

How can management consultants best be used in achieving good inventory control? The question is best answered at two levels: policy and technique. At the policy level, they can help the Board to clarify its attitude towards financial matters, especially in foreseeing the effects of investment in inventory on other facets of the company, and here a word of warning must be uttered. It is not always wise to expect outside consultants to *specify* the policy, though they should be encouraged to offer suggestions as to its formulation: since they should be *informed* suggestions, the consultant will often need to investigate the current state of affairs; this should be done with the co-operation of the company's own accountant, and sometimes its auditors as well, and always under the supervision of at least one member of the Board of Directors.

At the technique level, of course, consultants can be very helpful both in putting existing techniques to work, in modifying and adjusting them to suit the individual needs of a business and even, if they are the cream of the profession, in devising new 'tailor-made' systems specific to a company's unique requirements.

Conversely, there is a risk that low-grade consultants may try blindly to apply 'off-the-peg' methods which are not always appropriate, and therefore do more harm than good. One big company takes a harsh but realistic view of consultancy at the technique level as 'casual skilled professional labour'.

There are also two useful jobs that consultants can do which are closely related. One is that in moving around an organization they establish informal but none the less effective lines of communication which are 'cross-linkages' between departments at right angles to the usual vertical lines of authority. The other is that they can help to bring about changes in the organization. For example, Burns and Stalker[1] mention a case in the field of materials control—

> The production controller in Factory B had decided that the stock levels of a number of parts for his product were too low and had raised the minimum stock figures on the stores cards. Orders for making these

[1] T. BURNS and G. M. STALKER, *The Management of Innovation* (Tavistock Publications, 1961), page 84.

parts in numbers sufficient to meet these higher levels had been passed in routine fashion to the machine shop in Factory A, which had consequently found its monthly output programme abnormally high. Orders for metal stocks also rose, later on. The pressure on his machine-shop and the rise in material costs had mystified Production Controller A, since they were not apparently related to a comparable rise in the forecast of final units to be produced in either factory. Eventually, of course, Production Controller A had run the thing to earth, but there had been a period in which progress of work through his factory had been out of gear, when he had been unable to explain whence the increase in machine-shop time had come, and when he had been made to feel inefficient.

The recital of the salient points of this episode in this condensed fashion perhaps renders the difficulty too trivial and the solution too obvious. The common-sense response, only too clearly, is that if Production Controller B had only told Production Controller A what he was doing with the stores cards no trouble would ever have arisen.

Anyone who is considering the possible employment of management consultants in tackling his inventory problems would do well to remember that his choice is not confined to the Big Four and other members of the Management Consultants Association, but that a register is maintained by the British Institute of Management. Even this does not exhaust the possibilities for more and more academic institutions, technical colleges and universities alike, maintain departments of business studies, management science or operational research, the staff of which can often help an organization to sort out its stock control problems—and if they are cheaper than the established consultancy firms, this in no way implies technical inferiority. This and other germane points are well brought out in a competent little book on the subject.[1]

The Use of Computers

Much of the earlier part of this book showed that the technique of stock control could be reduced to sets of rules, once general policy decisions had been made. The junior staff who apply these rules need few qualities beyond reliability, application, and the ability to do arithmetic. They are the instruments of 'management by exception', filtering out the run-of-the-mill cases from the few unusual ones which call for the personal attention of the Materials Controller.

These requirements—reliability, application, and arithmetic—augmented by speed, are among the characteristics of computers, and such machines are well suited to the routine tasks of stock

[1] LAURA TATHAM, *The Efficiency Experts* (Business Publications, 1964).

control. The time they spend in actual computation (in commercial problems) is small in comparison with that taken in preparing the data for input and in translating the output. Because of this, the routine calculations which the computer performs on the data can be made much more complicated than those which it would be reasonable to submit to a human being. For example, we could arrange for the ROL's to be worked out afresh after each transaction instead of having a clerk revise them every three months or so, because the marginal cost of the extra calculation would be trivial.

Computers can also be used for sorting and bringing files up to date. With magnetic tapes as an auxiliary, they can record large quantities of information about stocks within a small compass and revise them with much less delay than in manual or punched-card systems. The IBM 'Ramac', which stores information on magnetic discs, takes half a second on the average to find and if necessary alter a single entry; the store contains about two million characters —about twelve times as many as there are in this book.

It is significant that whereas the earliest business applications of computers were almost automatically directed towards payroll calculations, there has more recently been a swing over to stock and production control as fields where the potential savings justify the expense of a computer. The emphasis has also shifted away from the saving in clerical labour to the wider benefits of more effective control.

The aircraft spares allocation quoted in Chapter 8 is an example of this; the amount of computing needed to determine the distribution of parts would just not have been feasible without the aid of a Univac I machine. Fig. 53 shows the computing plan which was drawn up, and Fig. 54 is a specimen of the output.

People tend to think of the electronic computer as a tool which only the largest companies can afford. This is not so. With the advent of computer service centres, their advantages can be applied to quite small companies. I have myself installed and operated a control system in this way; a manufacturing schedule was completed once a fortnight and took about twenty minutes of computer time. This cost £500 a year and made it possible to operate with a stock one-third lower than before, a capital saving of roughly £50,000. This is a useful sum to a small company—even taking a conservative interest rate of 5 per cent, the saving in stockholding cost is equivalent to five times the cost of computation. There are other advantages such as smoother operation of the plant and the ability to revise a complex schedule at short notice.

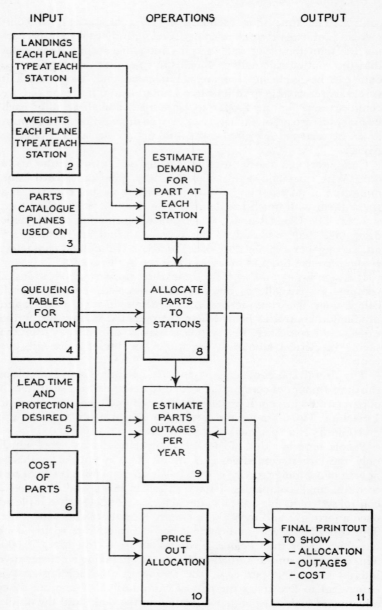

FIG 53 *Computing Plan for the Airlines Spare Parts Allocation*

PARTS-STATN	TWA PARTS ALLOCATION				FOREIGN					SUPPLY	
	1	2	3	4	5	6	7	8	9	10	11
0001–2209	0	0	0	0	0	0	0	0	0	0	0
0001–2212	0	0	0	0	0	0	0	0	0	0	0
0001–2213	0	0	0	0	0	0	0	0	0	0	0
0001–2214	0	0	0	0	0	0	0	0	0	0	0
0001–2215	0	0	0	0	0	0	0	0	0	0	0
0001–2216	0	0	0	0	0	1	0	0	0	0	1
0001–2217	0	0	0	0	0	0	0	0	0	0	1
0001–2218	0	0	0	0	0	1	0	0	0	0	1
0001–2222	0	0	0	0	0	0	0	0	0	0	0
0001–2223	0	0	0	0	0	0	0	0	0	0	0
0001–2224	0	0	0	0	0	0	0	0	0	0	0
0001–2225	0	0	0	0	0	0	0	0	0	0	0
0001–2227	0	0	0	0	0	0	0	0	0	0	0
0001–2228	0	0	0	0	0	0	0	0	0	0	0
0001–2229	0	0	0	0	0	0	0	0	0	0	0
0001–2235	0	0	0	0	0	0	0	0	0	0	0
0001–2237	0	0	0	0	0	0	0	0	0	0	0
0001–2241	0	0	0	0	0	0	0	0	0	0	0
0001–2242	0	0	0	0	0	0	0	0	0	0	0
0001–2243	0	0	0	0	0	0	0	0	0	0	0
0001–2244	0	0	0	0	0	1	0	0	0	1	1
0001–2247	0	0	0	0	0	0	0	0	0	0	0
0001–2249	0	0	0	0	0	0	0	0	0	0	0
0001–2250	0	0	0	0	0	0	0	0	0	0	0
0001–2255	0	0	0	0	0	0	0	0	0	0	0
0001–2265	0	0	0	0	0	1	0	0	1	1	1
0001–2275	0	1	0	0	0	1	0	0	1	1	1
0001–2279	0	0	0	0	0	1	0	0	1	1	1
0001–2280	0	0	0	0	0	0	0	0	0	0	0
0001–2509	0	0	0	0	0	0	0	0	0	0	0
0001–2513	0	0	0	0	0	0	0	0	0	0	0
0001–2524	0	0	0	0	0	0	0	0	0	0	0
0001–2528	0	0	0	0	0	0	0	0	0	0	0
0001–2530	0	0	0	0	0	0	0	0	0	0	0
0001–2532	0	0	0	0	0	0	0	0	0	0	0
0001–2603	0	0	0	0	0	0	0	0	0	0	0
0001–2700	0	0	0	0	0	1	0	0	1	1	1
0001–2701	0	0	0	0	0	0	0	0	0	0	0
0001–2775	0	0	0	0	0	0	0	0	0	0	0
0001–2802	0	0	0	0	0	0	0	0	0	0	0
0001–2804	0	0	0	0	0	0	0	0	0	0	0
0001–2810	0	0	0	0	0	0	0	0	0	0	0
0001–2825	0	0	0	0	0	0	0	0	0	0	0
0001–2826	0	0	0	0	0	0	0	0	0	0	0
0001–2852	0	1	0	1	1	1	0	0	1	1	1
0001–2853	1	1	1	1	1	1	0	0	1	1	2
0001–2854	0	0	0	0	0	1	0	0	1	1	1
0001–2855	0	0	0	0	0	0	0	0	0	0	1
0001–3001	0	0	0	0	0	1	0	0	1	1	1
0001–3002	0	0	0	0	0	1	0	0	1	1	1

FIG 54 *Spares Allocation: Sample of Output from Univac I Computer*

12	13	14	15	16	17	18	19	20	21	22	23	24
0	0	0	0	0	0	0	0	0	0	0	0	0
0	0	0	0	0	0	0	0	0	0	0	0	0
0	0	0	1	0	0	0	0	0	0	0	0	0
0	0	0	0	0	0	0	0	0	0	0	0	0
0	0	0	0	0	0	0	0	0	0	0	0	0
0	0	0	1	0	1	0	0	1	0	0	1	0
0	0	0	1	0	1	0	0	0	0	0	1	0
0	0	0	1	0	1	0	0	1	0	0	1	0
0	0	0	0	0	0	0	0	0	0	0	0	0
0	0	0	0	0	0	0	0	0	0	0	0	0
0	0	0	0	0	0	0	0	0	0	0	0	0
0	0	0	0	0	0	0	0	0	0	0	0	0
0	0	0	1	0	0	0	0	0	0	0	0	0
0	0	0	0	0	0	0	0	0	0	0	0	0
0	0	0	0	0	0	0	0	0	0	0	0	0
0	0	0	0	0	0	0	0	0	0	0	0	0
0	0	0	0	0	0	0	0	0	0	0	0	0
0	0	0	0	0	0	0	0	0	0	0	0	0
0	0	0	0	0	0	0	0	0	0	0	0	0
0	0	0	0	0	0	0	0	0	0	0	0	0
0	0	0	1	0	1	0	0	1	0	0	1	0
0	0	0	0	0	0	0	0	0	0	0	0	0
0	0	0	0	0	0	0	0	0	0	0	0	0
0	0	0	0	0	0	0	0	0	0	0	0	0
0	0	0	0	0	0	0	0	0	0	0	0	0
1	1	1	1	0	1	1	1	1	0	1	1	0
1	1	1	1	0	1	1	1	1	0	1	1	0
0	0	0	1	0	1	0	0	1	0	0	1	0
0	0	0	0	0	0	0	0	0	0	0	0	0
0	0	0	0	0	0	0	0	0	0	0	0	0
0	0	0	0	0	0	0	0	0	0	0	0	0
0	0	0	0	0	0	0	0	0	0	0	0	0
0	0	0	0	0	0	0	0	0	0	0	0	0
0	0	0	0	0	0	0	0	0	0	0	0	0
0	0	0	0	0	0	0	0	0	0	0	0	0
0	0	0	0	0	0	0	0	0	0	0	0	0
0	0	0	1	0	1	0	0	1	0	0	1	0
0	0	0	0	0	0	0	0	0	0	0	0	0
0	0	0	0	0	0	0	0	0	0	0	0	0
0	0	0	0	0	0	0	0	0	0	0	0	0
0	0	0	0	0	0	0	0	0	0	0	0	0
0	0	0	0	0	0	0	0	0	0	0	0	0
0	0	0	0	0	0	0	0	0	0	0	0	0
0	0	0	1	0	1	0	0	0	0	0	0	0
1	1	1	2	0	1	1	1	1	0	1	1	0
1	1	1	3	0	2	1	1	2	0	1	2	0
0	0	0	1	0	1	0	0	1	0	0	1	0
0	0	0	1	0	1	0	0	0	0	0	1	0
1	1	1	1	0	1	1	1	1	0	1	1	0
0	0	0	1	0	1	0	0	1	0	0	1	0

FIG 54 (cont'd).

The cost of computing has fallen to about a tenth of what it was a decade ago and computer methods seem likely to go on developing, with correspondingly greater savings by tighter control of inventories.

Three contributors to more efficient computing are the organization of the computing facility itself, better peripheral equipment and improved systems of data collection and transmission.

Trends in Computing Equipment

Computers themselves have changed: the hardware has become more obviously separated into central processing units (C.P.U.) and peripherals. The latter consist in the main of machines which 'read' and 'write', whereas the CPU's actually process the information. CPU's have become faster—so fast that speeds once measured in thousands of a second are now measured in millionths; even the microsecond is not always a conveniently small enough unit and may have to give way to the nanosecond (one thousand millionth) or even the picasecond (a million millionth part of one second). They have also become bigger. The trend seems to be away from the company-owned or company-rented machine towards a communal one serving several customers under a 'time-sharing' system. The machine thus operates in much the same way as a public utility, connected to its users through the telephone or Telex network; so cheap has this sort of computing become that the cost of the telephone call is a significantly large part of it.

Each of the users will have his own 'terminal', a piece of peripheral equipment through which he communicates with a CPU; the latter has its own automatic data storage and work-scheduling arrangements, designed to maintain an efficient service by ensuring that the central machine is kept occupied with a steady flow of work. Such terminals are still, in the main, slow and noisy teleprinters, but they are unlikely to remain so. Messages from the machine to the user may now be displayed on the screen of a cathode ray tube rather like a television set, though unlike a television set in that devices such as touchwires or a light pen enable the viewer to ask questions eliciting more detailed information.

Most input is through keyboards, but the tedium of punching cards or paper tape is being overcome as the data go in via high-speed magnetic tapes or discs, or direct into the machine's 'buffer store'. Even these obsolescing hand-written documents are scanned by Magnetic Ink Character Recognition (MICR, already familiar in association with bank cheques) and Optical Character Recognition (OCR).

6

In the future, not too far distant, automated stores will use sensing devices, so that stocks, especially weighable ones like small spares, will be continuously monitored and, if desired, re-ordered automatically. The automation has already progressed to the extent that even the handling of the goods into and out of store is integrated with the electronic recording of their movements and the preparation of the relevant documents. Such a system has already been developed by the Industrial Systems Division of Aerojet-General (see *Computer Weekly*, 18.12.69) but of course the entire warehouse with its stacking crane was designed around the computing machinery. But there will always be at least one human being somewhere in the system: it is well to remember that one early attempt at a giant centrally-computed inventory control system—in NAAFI—came to grief because it did not take enough cognizance of human weakness in its operators.

Before concluding, it would perhaps be useful to give a brief survey of certain Professional Bodies whose activities, publications, examinations, etc., are relevant to the contents of this book and may therefore be of interest to the reader.

Operational Research Society

Operational research came into being in the years before World War II, when a few scientists began to apply their methods of formal analysis to military problems. Their success was such that when the war was over, they turned naturally to industrial problems, following the tradition of F. W. Taylor and the 'scientific management' movement of which he is generally accepted as the father. British operational researchers formed a club which coalesced into a formal society in the early 1950's and is now a thriving professional organization. In the decade from 1957 to 1967, its membership increased sixfold and it now has more than two thousand members in the United Kingdom. The Society's journal, the *Operational Research Quarterly*, publishes excellent papers, mainly with a strong mathematical content but much more practical, in the main, than those of the corresponding societies in the U.S.A. and other foreign countries.

Many of its members are interested in stock control: a recent survey showed that the proportion was 45 per cent and the Society has a study group devoted to Production and Inventory Control. In neither Operational Research in general nor Inventory Control in particular does the Operational Research Society offer formal qualifications, but membership is carefully regulated, is already recognized as bestowing some distinction upon those whose skill permits their entry, and will almost certainly become an official badge of competence within a few years. The Society has its office at 62 Cannon Street, London, E.C.4 and details of its activities may be obtained from the Secretary at that address.

Similar in its scope and membership is The Institute of Management Science (*TIMS*), of American origin but with international interests. Its journal, *Management Science*, also includes papers on the theory of inventory control and a U.K. Chapter of TIMS was founded in 1968.

A.P.I.C.S. and B.P.I.C.S.

These initials denote respectively the American and British Production and Inventory Control Societies, the latter being the only one in the United Kingdom to specialize in these two closely related subjects. It began as the London and Scottish chapters of its American affiliate but emerged as a Society in its own right in 1969. *BPICS* runs an annual Technical Conference, publishes the Proceedings of each as well as issuing a monthly newsletter and making the *APICS* publications available to its members: the latter include a quarterly journal, *Production and Inventory Management*, a dictionary of technical terms, special reports and training manuals.

The Institute of Purchasing and Supply

The Institute of Purchasing and Supply was formed in 1967 by a merger of the Purchasing Officers Association and the Institute of Public Supplies, both parent bodies having contributed to the advancement of stock control as well as other aspects of materials control; the latter now tends to be known increasingly as 'the supply function'. It publishes much interesting and relevant matter including *Purchasing Journal* (monthly).[1]

Membership (M.Inst.P.S.) amd Fellowship (F.Inst.P.S.) are recognized professional qualifications and the examination syllabus includes Stores Management and Inventory Control as a prominent feature.

The Institute has a strong interest in education, which extends to the award, by examination, of a *Certificate in Storekeeping* available to "any person engaged in Stores, Stock Control, Stores Accounting or any associated function". This certificate is unique and it requires evidence of practical experience as well as a very broad field of study.

[1] For details write to the Editor at the Institute's headquarters, York House, Westminster Bridge Road, London, S.E.1.

Summary

We have come to the end of a survey of stock control which may seem to have expounded more questions than it answers. I think that this truly reflects our present situation—we whose business it is to

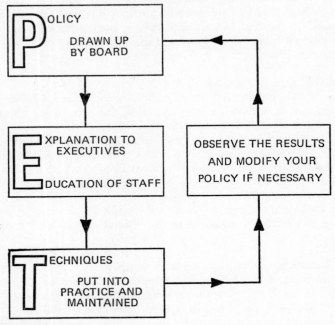

Fig 55 *The PET Theory*

seek the answers are only too well aware of our present inadequacies. Nevertheless, we are also aware of the enormous savings which *could* be made by applying even the few simple methods outlined in this book.

Many attempts at installing scientific stock control come to grief because an enthusiastic stock controller, newly converted to statistics, rushes in with a Pandora's Box of techniques unsupported by policy decisions at the highest level. The sequence should always follow the PET theory shown in Fig. 55, which is important enough to be repeated here in the text. Set your POLICY first; EXPLAIN it to your executives and EDUCATE your staff according to that policy; give them the TECHNIQUES to achieve it and you will help to turn some of the superfluous fat of industry into the energy of productive resources.

Finally, never forget that the most widely useful method in the whole field of stock control is common sense. It is fitting to conclude with these words of T. H. Huxley—

> Science is nothing but trained and organized common sense, differing from the latter only as a veteran may differ from a raw recruit: and its methods differ from those of common sense only as far as the guardsman's cut and thrust differ from the manner in which a savage wields his club.

Exercise

(1) In what fundamental way does an information store differ from a stock of material?

APPENDIX 1

What is a Stock?

I on the Questions taire them tightly.
ROBERT BURNS, *The Inventory.*

We mentioned in Chapter 1 the difficulty of deciding what to include in a stock centre and what to leave out. To illustrate the general approach to this problem, let us take the mythical chemical product, mephistophelene. The Work Study Department has compiled a flow process chart of its manufacture: part of this is reproduced in Fig. 56.

For conventional accounting, our stock of finished product would simply be that in store (storage 12 on the chart). Is this figure a suitable assessment of the buffer stock? What we must realize is that Fig. 56 represents the process in a state of *normality*, whereas our greatest interest in buffer stocks occurs during states of *emergency*, when they are at their lowest. When in a hurry, we should not be inclined to wait for test results (delay 8) but get on with the job and risk having to reject the material later. Material from the bagging machine would go straight to the loading platform with no inter-mediate storage, and delay 15 would be cut out by having a lorry ready immediately.

Next we must look at the procedure for accepting orders. The Sales Manager tells us, "If I get an urgent order by telephone, I must be able to fill it *immediately.*" He never can, of course: it takes nearly an hour to mark and load up an order for one ton. Pressed for a more precise answer, the Sales Manager says, "I mean that if a customer rings me up before lunch, I want the order to be on its way that same afternoon." This gives us, let us say, five hours' grace: allowing an hour for marking and loading we are left with a critical period of four hours. We can expect material which has not even been milled yet to arrive within this critical period. Since the mill takes ten hundredweights at a time, we can add this quantity at least to our finished stock. The stock boundaries, then, are five hours apart: the input finishes at operation 4 and the output begins at transport 17.

You will recognize this as the sort of common-sense assessment

MANUFACTURE OF MEPHISTOPHELENE:
PART OF MATERIAL-TYPE FLOW PROCESS CHART

PROCESS TIME

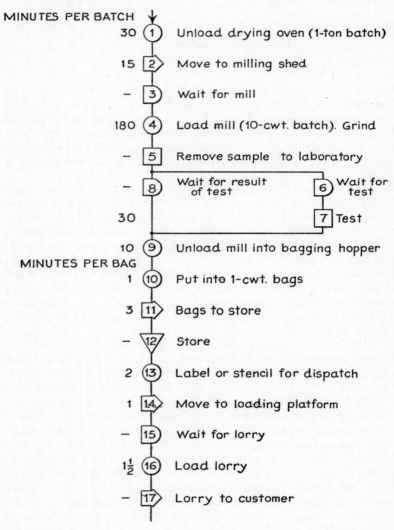

MINUTES PER BATCH		
30	(1)	Unload drying oven (1-ton batch)
15	[2]	Move to milling shed
–	[3]	Wait for mill
180	(4)	Load mill (10-cwt. batch). Grind
–	[5]	Remove sample to laboratory
–	[8]	Wait for result of test [6] Wait for test
30		[7] Test
10	(9)	Unload mill into bagging hopper

MINUTES PER BAG

1	(10)	Put into 1-cwt. bags
3	[11]	Bags to store
–	▽12	Store
2	(13)	Label or stencil for dispatch
1	[14]	Move to loading platform
–	[15]	Wait for lorry
1½	(16)	Load lorry
–	[17]	Lorry to customer

FIG 56

which goes on in any factory, when the staff, who are reasonable and co-operative human beings, are faced with an urgent situation.

One important principle which emerges is that the 'stock boundaries' for *buffer stocks* should be set according to abnormal or emergency conditions. Another is that these boundaries may be defined in different ways for different purposes. We have already mentioned how a formal accounting procedure would accept only storage 12 on the chart as a rigid definition of finished stock. There may also be the legal definition to consider, our stock then including material in the customer's own warehouse if it has not yet been paid for; there is a good case for including 'Accounts Receivable' as a stockholding cost. The accountants' convention of lumping 'Stocks and Debtors' together, as a single item in a balance sheet, also looks logical from this point of view.

There is a practical side to boundary-setting, as one contributor to the international buffer stock of tin (Nigeria) found to its advantage. When the agreement was re-negotiated so as to require a greater contribution of metallic tin, the latter was achieved simply by redefining the stock boundary so that it came to include certain stocks held in warehouses at ports.

In applying Method Study to compile Fig. 56, we used the five standard ASME symbols. Work Study practitioners have worried and argued for some time over the difference between the D used for 'delay' and the inverted triangle which denotes 'storage'. This vexed question can now be answered in stock control terms by reference back to Chapter 1: 'storage' is purposeful and 'delay' is accidental and therefore wasteful. It follows that the good work study man will try to eliminate his delays but to *design* his storages. I have argued elsewhere[1] that the new methods of management science are the legitimate tools of the work study investigator, and scientific stock control is now seen to be one of them. However, the flow of useful information need not be entirely in one direction, as this Appendix shows.

We can also learn a good deal about our more important stocks by using the systematic questioning technique system of Work Study. A possible scheme is given below: it is not intended to be exhaustive, but an investigator who works through this list should be in a good position to follow through with his own subsidiary questions. Asterisks indicate questions for which the advice of a statistician or other specialist may be needed.

[1] BATTERSBY, A., "The Use of established O.R. techniques in work study" *Work Study and Management* (Sept., 1963) *7*, 392.

WHY is this stock held?
>   Is it   (a) accidental?
>   (b) purposeful?

If (a), how frequently do such accidents happen? should provision for them be made a matter of routine? If so, they will become purposeful. If not, look into the nature of the accident which gave rise to the stock. This WHY is repeated in greater detail below but still needs to be asked FIRST. Many of the 'why' questions may be translated into—

WHAT is this stock?
>   Description—
>>   Name of material
>>   Finished product?
>>   Partly processed or intermediate product?
>>   Raw material?
>>   Product of one process which serves as raw material for
>>   another?
>>   Waste for disposal?
>>   Special characteristics, e.g. bonded stock
>   Specification—
>>   Grade of material
>>   Limits of impurities, dimensions, etc.
>>   Passed inspection or rejected for rectification?
>>   Storage life
>>   Fashionable? perishable? obsolescent? obsolete?
>   Identification—
>>   Batch number, etc.
>   Value—
>>   Standard or actual
>>   Material or works cost
>>   Selling price
>>   Possibility of changes in value through fashion or perishability
>>   or obsolescence
>>   Cost of containers
>   Boundaries—
>>   Define the exact points in the process at which material enters
>>   or leaves the stock

*WHY is it held?
>   Absorbing fluctuations in—

Sales	(a)	random, short-term
	(b)	seasonal
	(c)	long-term
Production	(a)	cycle
	(b)	breakdowns, spoilt batches and other un-certainties
	(c)	work load 1. Machines
		2. Men
Raw Materials	(a)	delivery, availability

     (*b*) reliability, possibility of rejection
     (*c*) strategic
Examine all these under the general headings
     (i) quantity
     (ii) quality
     (iii) price

WHEN?
     Date manufactured
     Date ordered
     Date received into stock
     Date packed or prepared for dispatch
     Date due for dispatch
     Note any unusual delays which do not appear to fit the normal
         pattern

WHO is responsible for it?
     Responsibility for—
     (*a*) adding to stock
     (*b*) taking from stock
     (*c*) transferring from one stock to another, e.g. re-grading
     (*d*) storage and handling
     (*e*) recording, inspection, insurance, special treatment (e.g.
         keeping rats away)
     Distinguish between—
     (i) day-to-day (tactical) decisions
     (ii) policy (strategic) decisions
Is more than one person responsible for each activity?

HOW is it stored?
     Type of storage—
     Bulk (open storage, silos, sheds, bins, tanks, etc.)
     Packages (bags, drums, barrels, cases, etc.)
     Heated? Refrigerated? Air-conditioned?
     Protected against pilferage?
         leading to estimates* of the costs of storage
     Methods of handling
     By conventional Work Study investigations, again leading to
         cost estimates*
     How much?
     Is storage capacity (*a*) freely available?
                      (*b*) just adequate?
                      (*c*) inadequate?
     Do we own or rent it?

WHERE is it held?
     (Again, many of the questions under this heading are implied by
         some of those already given)
     Is it—
     (*a*) all in one place?
     (*b*) spread about?

If (*a*), is it—
    (*c*) near to the input process?
    (*d*) near to the output process?
    (*e*) near to neither?
As regards security, is it—
    (*f*) open to pilferage?
    (*g*) accessible to a determined thief?
    (*h*) well protected?
    (*k*) guarded?
    (*l*) bonded?

These questions should be supplemented by those which search for alternatives, after which the alternatives should be critically examined, following the usual Method Study procedure.[1]

[1] See FIELDS, A., *Method Study* (Cassell, 1969).

APPENDIX 2

Finding Economic Lot Sizes when the Number of Orders is Fixed

The firm of Tam O'Shanter Ltd. deals in the following five items, of which the costs and sales are given—

Name of Item	Cost per Item, £	Sales per Week		ELS	ONO
		Number	Value £		
Skellums	25	50	1,250	28	1·77
Melders	5	100	500	90	1·12
Meikle Stanes	30	150	4,500	45	3·35
Winnock-Bunkers	2	300	600	245	1·22
Cummocks	1	600	600	490	1·22
		Totals	7,450	898	8·68

The Economic Lot Size (ELS) and Optimum Number of Orders (ONO) are given for each item, and are based on the same assumptions as in Chapter 2, i.e. an ordering cost of about £1 and a rate of return on capital of $\frac{1}{2}$ per cent per week. However, the total number of orders to be placed comes out at about nine per week, whereas the capacity of the Buying Department is known to be thirty orders per week. Not only are there mathematical restrictions on the ONO calculations but practical ones as well, for the Buying Department costs £30 a week to run, and no real saving occurs in the administrative costs if by placing only nine orders weekly, the Department were utilized to less than one third of its full capacity. Even an arbitrary allocation of six orders per item will lower the general level of stock, as the table on page 158 shows.

The best allocation of orders can be found by a stepwise calculation. Having divided the orders equally amongst the five products, we have six orders for each product. Since we need 600 cummocks a week, each order will be for 100, and the average stock will be 50 items, value £50. We calculate this stock value for all five products as shown above.

The ordering cost is constant at £30, so our aim will be to reduce

157

Item	(1) Sales	(2) Cost	(3) Sales Value (1) × (2)	(4) Half Sales (3) ÷ (2)	(5) No. of Orders	(6) Stock Value (4) ÷ (5)
		£	£	£		£
Skellums	50	25	1,250	625	6	104·20
Melders	100	5		250	6	41·70
M-Stanes	150	30	4,500	2,250	6	375·00
W-Bunkers	300	2	600	300	6	50·00
Cummocks	600	1	600	300	6	50·00
				Total	30	£620·90

the total investment in stock from £620·60 to the lowest possible value.

The average stock value for cummocks is £50. By placing five orders instead of six, this value would become £60, an increase of £10. On the other hand, seven orders would give a stock value of £42·90, a decrease of £7·10. We arrive at the next table by making the same calculation for all the products—

Item	No. of Orders	Placing One Less Order Will Increase the Stock Value by	Placing One More Order Will Decrease the Stock Value by
		£	£
Skellums	6	20·80	14·90
Melders	6	8·30*	6·00
M-Stanes	6	75·00	53·60*
W-Bunkers	6	10·00	7·10
Cummocks	6	10·00	7·10

This shows clearly that if we transfer one order from melders to meikle-stanes we shall reduce the stock of the latter by £53·60, while the former increases by only £8·30. By matching the lowest entry in the third column (marked with an asterisk) with the highest in the

Item	No. of Orders	Placing One Less Order Will Increase the Stock Value by	Placing One More Order Will Decrease the Stock Value by
		£	£
Skellums	6	20·80	14·90
Melders	5	12·50	8·30
M-Stanes	7	53·60	40·20*
W-Bunkers	6	10·00*	7·10
Cummocks	6	10·00*	7·10

last column (also marked) we get the maximum effect from re-allocating one order; it reduces the total investment in stock by £45·30.

Now we draw up a second table in the same way, beginning with the new allocation of orders (see table on previous page).

This shows us that we should transfer one order from winnock-bunkers or cummocks to meikle-stanes, reducing the total investment in stock by £30·20. By continuing in this way we eventually reach the following allocation—

Item	No. of Orders	Placing One Less Order Will Increase the Stock Value by £	Placing One More Order Will Decrease the Stock Value by £
Skellums	6	20·80	14·90
Melders	4	20·80*	12·50
M-Stanes	12	17·10*	14·40
W-Bunkers	4	25·00	15·00*
Cummocks	4	25·00	15·00*

No figure in the third column is less than any in the fourth column; this means any further re-allocation of orders must of necessity increase the total stock value, which at this point has fallen to £504·20. This allocation is therefore the most economic one.

The Buyer knows that with one extra typist at £6 a week his department could deal with 36 orders a week. Should he engage her?

We must find out whether we can save the same amount. First we find the allocation of the extra six orders; the last column of the last table above shows that the first of these extra orders should be for winnock-bunkers and cummocks, one to each. We then recalculate the last column only—

Item	No. of Orders	Placing One More Order Will Decrease the Stock Value by £
Skellums	6	14·90*
Melders	4	12·50
M-Stanes	12	14·40
W-Bunkers	5	10·00
Cummocks	5	10·00

and give an extra order to skellums.

The final allocation of the 36 orders is—

Item	No. of Orders	Average Stock Value £
Skellums	7	89·30
Melders	5	50·00
M-Stanes	14	160·70
W-Bunkers	5	60·00
Cummocks	5	60·00
Total	36	£420·00

So the extra six orders will reduce our investment in stock from £504·20 to £420. The difference of £84·20 at ½ per cent per week represents a saving of only £0·42, so the Buyer cannot justify engaging the extra typist.

APPENDIX 3

The Effect of Quantity Discounts
on Economic Lot Sizes

We have found the economic lot size to be 400 tons for chocolic acid
at £0·25 a ton when sales are 100 tons a week. Suppose the supplier
were to offer us a discount of £0·01 a ton for lots of 500 tons or
more—what then?

The discount would reduce the price by £1·00 a week. If we were
to order in 500-ton lots we should have an average stock of 250 tons.
This would be worth £57·50, and at ½ per cent per week would
give us a stockholding cost of £0·29 a week. The cost of ordering
would be £0·19 a week, making a total of £0·48. The 500-ton lots
are cheaper, as the following table shows—

Lot Size:	400 tons	500 tons
Price per Ton	£0·24	£0·23
Sales Rate	100 tons /wk.	100 tons/wk.
Costs per Week—		
	£	£
Purchasing Price	24·00	23·00
Stockholding Cost	0·24	0·29
Ordering Cost	0·24	0·19
TOTAL COST PER WEEK	£24·48	£23·48
Difference		£1·00

We now ask whether it would be even cheaper to increase the lot
size still more. There is a simple rule for answering this. If the stockholding cost at the discount level (ignoring buffer stock) is greater
than the ordering cost, the economic batch size remains at the discount level; if the stockholding cost is lower, we must work out a new
economic lot size at the discount price. In this example, the stockholding cost at £0·29 is greater than the ordering cost at £0·19, so
we order lots of 500 tons and no more.

It so happens that the economic lot size at the discount price is
409 tons. The discount level is higher than this and it is obvious that

161

to increase our lot size would increase the total cost. A glance at Fig. 7 will make this clear. When we are in the region to the right of the economic lot size, the stockholding cost is higher than the ordering cost, and increases faster than the corresponding decreases in the ordering cost.

If the supplier were now to offer you a further discount of a penny on lots of 1,000 tons or more, would you accept it?

Economic Lot Sizes for Three Products Manufactured in Series

We have an assembly plant which is producing three products one after the other; they are—

Product	Cost per Item £	Sales per Week
Washing Machines	20	25
Waste Disposers	10	50
Refrigerators	20	75
		150

The plant can produce 150 items a week; this rate is the same for all the products, so production and sales are exactly balanced. It costs £20 to change the plant over from any product to any other product and we can arrange the change-over so that it causes no loss of production. If we value our capital at ½ per cent per week, what is the economic lot size for each product?

We shall begin by assuming (for the reasons given in Chapter 2) that the lot sizes are directly proportional to the rates of sale and that the three products follow each other in a manufacturing *cycle*. The problem is now to find the most economical cycle period.

Let us look first at the change-over costs (equivalent to the ordering cost); in any one cycle, we change the product three times, so the total cost is £60. The cost per week is this £60 divided by the number of weeks for which the cycle lasts.

Next we consider the stocks, and here a complication arises. The products we 'order' do not arrive in one single consignment, but in a steady flow. While they are flowing in from the production line, they are also flowing out to customers. Take washing machines as an example; in any one week we can make 150 but shall sell 25, so our stock will increase by only 125, which is five-sixths of the number produced. This factor is easily calculated—

163

(1) Divide the sales rate by the production rate.

(2) Subtract the result from one.

The factors in respect of the three products under consideration are as follows—

Washing Machines	$\frac{5}{6}$ i.e.	0·833
Waste Disposers	$\frac{2}{3}$ i.e.	0·667
Refrigerators	$\frac{1}{2}$ i.e.	0·500

Suppose for the moment that our manufacturing cycle lasts for a week. Then the average cycle stocks and their values would be—

Item	(1) No. Made	(2) Factor	(3) Max. Stock (1) × (2)	(4) Avge. Stock (3) ÷ 2	(5) Unit Value £	(6) Cycle Stock Value (4) × (5) £
Washing Machines	25	0·833	20·83	10·42	20	208
Waste Disposers	50	0·667	33·33	16·67	10	167
Refrigerators	75	0·500	37·50	18·75	20	375

Total Value of Cycle stocks   £750

Stockholding cost at $\frac{1}{2}$% = £3·75 a week

It is obvious that for a cycle of two weeks the stockholding cost would be doubled, and so on. We can now draw up a table of costs for various cycle periods—

Weeks	Change-over £	Stockholding £	Total £
1	60·00	3·75	63·75
2	30·00	7·50	37·50
3	20·00	11·25	31·25
4*	15·00	15·00	30·00*
5	12·00	18·75	30·75
6	10·00	22·50	32·50
7	8·57	26·25	34·82
8	7·50	30·00	37·50

The economic cycle period is four weeks, when the change-over and stockholding costs are each equal to £15.

The cycle period may be found directly in the following way—

1. Calculate the total change-over cost for one cycle (£60).

2. Calculate the stockholding cost per week for a one-week cycle (£3·75).

3. Divide the former by the latter (16).

4. Take the square root (4).

Once we know that the cycle period is 4 weeks, we can readily find the economic lot sizes for the individual products; as it happens, they turn out to be exactly equal to the monthly sales—

Washing Machines	100	(110)
Waste Disposers	200	(245)
Refrigerators	300	(245)

(The figures in brackets are those which we found by the square-root law and gave in Table IV on page 30. In working them out, the effect of selling and producing at the same time was allowed for by using the factors already given; the method of doing this is to divide the sales rate by the factor before using it to calculate the lot size.)

Figs. 57 and 58 give an interesting comparison between the two sets of figures. Fig. 57 shows how the square-root law gives a manufacturing cycle which throws the stocks more and more out of

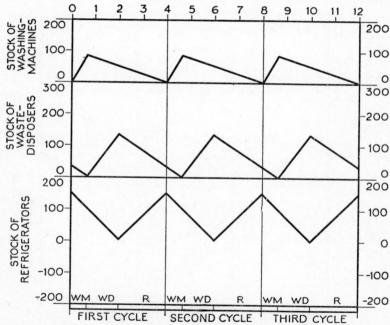

FIG 57 *Manufacture of Three Products in Series: Incorrect Lot Sizes Found by the Square-Root Law*

balance. Fig. 58, based on the figures calculated in this appendix, shows a stable cycle which can be repeated indefinitely.

Two other interesting facts about the cycle in Fig. 58 are worth mentioning. First, the average stocks of the three products are—

			£
Washing Machines	42	worth	840
Waste Disposers	67	worth	670
Refrigerators	75	worth	1,500
Total	184	worth	3,010

Allowing for rounding errors, the stockholding cost at $\frac{1}{2}$ per cent would be £15, as we have already shown. Although the total value of the stock varies a little during the cycle, the total number of items remains the same at 184. The proportions of the three products change, but their total does not. This is called the 'cycle stock' or 'carry-over stock' and it is directly proportional to the length of the cycle.

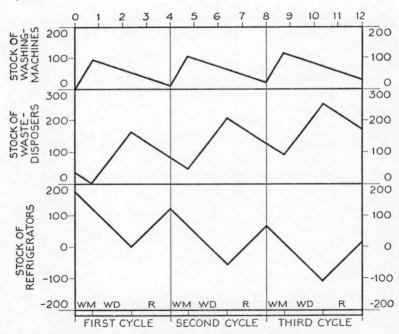

FIG 58 *Manufacture of Three Products in Series: Lot Sizes in a Balanced Economic Cycle*

The second point is this. We have assumed a very simple cycle in which each product is made once only: if we split one of the runs, might we produce a still cheaper cycle? It seems logical to divide the run of refrigerators, since it is the longest. This turns out to be more complicated than you might think, because the best 'split-run' cycle contains two *unequal* runs of refrigerators, as illustrated in Fig. 59. The cycle period has lengthened to 5·24 weeks; the total cost is £30·55, so splitting the run has actually increased the cost.

We could go on trying out other variations, but enough has already been said to show how the simple square-root law becomes hopelessly inadequate in situations of this sort.

What is the square root of 3?

$$3 = 300 \div 100$$

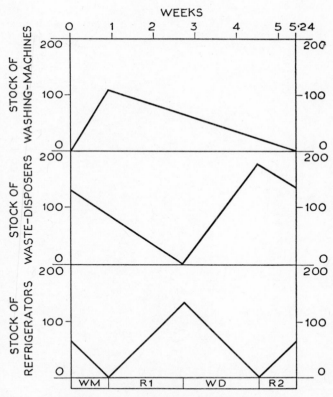

FIG 59 *Manufacture of Three Products in Series: Best 'Split-run' Cycle*

The table gives the square root of 300 as 17, so divide this by ten to get 1·7 as the approximate square root of 3 (a more exact value is 1·732).

A more accurate value may be obtained by dividing the number by its square root as found from the table, then taking the average of the divisor and the quotient. The table gives 17 as the square root of 300

$$300 \div 17 = 17 \cdot 6$$
$$\text{Average} = 17 \cdot 3$$

A Short Table of Square Roots

Number		Square
From	To	Root
100	110	10
111	132	11
133	156	12
157	192	13
193	200	14
200	210	14
211	240	15
241	272	16
273	300	17
300	306	17
307	342	18
343	380	19
381	400	20
400	420	20
421	462	21
463	500	22
500	506	22
507	552	23
553	600	24
600	—	24
601	650	25
651	700	26
700	756	27
757	800	28
800	812	28
813	870	29
871	900	30

Number		Square
From	To	Root
900	930	30
931	992	31
993	1000	32

Examples of Use

The range of numbers given in the two left-hand columns under Number is *inclusive*, so the square root of 211 is 15 and the square root of 552 is 23, in both cases to the nearest whole number.

Numbers outside the ranges given may be multiplied or divided by 100.

Solutions to Exercises

CHAPTER 2
1. 5 gross
2. Each is 3·75 new pence
3. 4 gross or 5 gross
4. 4·5p
5. It would not change
6. 60 to 90 wing-nuts per month
7. A— 9 orders
   B— 7 ,,
   C— 2 ,,
   D— 9 ,,
   E— 9 ,,
   F—24 ,,
   Value of stock £82·09
8. 20 orders a year

In case the use of decimal currency has caused confusion, the individual steps for calculating the ONO are given below.
Units: pounds, years, per cent per annum.
   (1) $0·90 \times 200 = 180$
   (2) $20 \div 180 = 1/9$
   (3) Constant $= \sqrt{1/9} = 1/3$
   (4) Turnover $= 1200 \times 3 = 3600$
   (5) ONO $= 1/3 \times \sqrt{3600} = 20$

CHAPTER 3
1. 30 tons is two standard deviations above the mean, so the answer is one week in fifty or roughly once a year.
2. Sixty-eight.

CHAPTER 4
1. Because although the buffer stock and therefore the ROL depend on the lead time, the ROQ does not. In any case, the lead time is not necessarily the same as the delivery time.

2. $40 \times 1\cdot732 = 69$ tons

3, Assuming a 2 per cent risk level, we have for diabolone—

$$2 \times \text{Standard Deviation} = 2 \times 5 \text{ tons}$$
$$= 10 \text{ tons}$$
$$\sqrt{2} \times 10 = 14 \text{ tons}$$

Since the Normal distribution is symmetrical, this figure is the same for the negative and positive buffer stocks.

CHAPTER 5

1. (*a*) $1/4(96 + 129 + 69 + 194) = \dfrac{488}{4} = 122\cdot0$

   (*b*) $1/13(1298 - 131 + 194) = \dfrac{1361}{13} = 104\cdot7$

   (*c*) $1/52(5032 - 76 + 194) = \dfrac{5150}{52} = 98\cdot0$

2. Old forecast = Average for 1971 = 97
   (*a*) $0\cdot60 \times 97 + 0\cdot40 \times 194 = 58\cdot2 + 77\cdot6 = 135\cdot8$
   (*b*) $0\cdot86 \times 97 + 0\cdot14 \times 194 = 83\cdot4 + 27\cdot2 = 110\cdot6$
   (*c*) $0\cdot96 \times 97 + 0\cdot04 \times 194 = 93\cdot1 + 7\cdot8 = 100\cdot9$

CHAPTER 6

1. The buffer stock for a one-month lead time, at the 2 per cent risk level, would be 30 tons (twice the standard deviation); for nine months it would be $3 \times 30 = 90$ tons. The expected sales during nine months are 540 tons, so the ROL is 630 tons.

The ROQ cannot be determined without further data.

CHAPTER 10

1. There is no Law of Conservation of Information: you can withdraw as much information as you like without depleting the stock.

Index

173